Fear Not

You Have Favor With God

by Reverend Glenda Carlson

PRESS

Fear Not
You Have Favor With God
by Rev. Glenda Carlson

Printed in the United States of America

ISBN 9781612155500

Unless otherwise indicated, Bible quotations are taken from The King James Version of the Bible.

www.xulonpress.com

Endorsements

*F*ear Not: You Have Favor With God *is thought-pro-voking and hope-producing. It reminds us that despite what we have or have not done in the past, God's forgiveness will set us free and alleviate our spiritual, mental, and emotional suffering. It also reminds us not to allow Satan to steal our joy by continuing to carry the shame of the past.

Darlene J. Brantley, LBSW, MS
Counselor of Wiregrass Hospice,
Dothan, Alabama

In this publication, the author gives God honor and praises for bringing her through many situations in her life which seemed impossible at the time. Through it all, He allowed her to grow strong in the Holy Spirit and to share in His powerful anointing. As a minister, I recognize that a meaningful ministering tool has been developed through this Scripturally-based composition.

Rev. John Baxter, retired High School Principal,
former Band Director and Minister of Music,
as well as current Pastor of Providence United
Methodist Church, Geneva, Alabama

Glenda Carlson's manuscript *Fear Not: You Have Favor With God* is an excellent value to the Christian world, as well as those who are not Christians, but need to become so. Mrs. Carlson adds a personal touch throughout the manuscript of her experiences, which encourages readers to stay focused on the Lord. She also includes helpful lessons that apply to everyday life. The greatest influence of the manuscript is the solid, Biblically-based applications, which are so very important for Christian growth in the Word. Mrs. Carlson's book encourages the reader not to give up, even in the worst of times. She reminds the reader that God is able to solve their biggest problems. I would greatly recommend this book to all audiences. I know that God will use it for His glory. I'm thankful to have been able to read it.

Barbara Lee, Editor

This Book Is Dedicated To

B rent, my youngest son, who grew up in California, but now lives in Hawaii. I praise God for his sweet, gentle, forgiving spirit. I praise God that he is a living, walking, breathing miracle today because of God's supernatural power.

Paris, my first son, who is nine years older than his brother. I praise God that he is learning to become more than a conqueror through Christ. I praise God that he, too, is a living, walking, breathing miracle straight from Almighty God.

Ocie, my dear sweet, precious mother, who went home to be with the Lord in November of 2002. How I cherish the six years we had together, as I took care of her. She loved the Lord and she loved her family and church family.

Claude, my earthly father, who has also gone on to be with the Lord. I now realize that he loved me and he did the best he could to show it.

Dwayne, my wonderful husband, who loves me and believes in me and in what God is doing in me, for me, and through me as I learn to fully trust in God.

ACKNOWLEDGEMENTS

The following people have played a major role in my life by inspiring and encouraging me along my journey:

1. Dr. Paul Walker, former pastor of Mt. Paran Church of God, Atlanta, Georgia, now serving on a national executive level.

2. Trinity Broadcasting Network, and Jan and Paul Crouch, for their humble dedication to, and persistence in, spreading the Word of God all around the world.

3. Rev. James Robison, a dynamic Spirit-filled minister of the Gospel, who makes me think of Jeremiah, the weeping prophet, full of compassion for people.

4. Rev. John Baxter, pastor of Providence United Methodist Church in Geneva, Alabama, who is

my pastor and mentor and whom I dearly love and respect.

5. Rev. Marilyn Hickey, an exhilarating spirit filled woman of God still going strong after all these years.

6. Rev. Paula White, a dynamic Spirit-filled woman of God who never seems to lose her enthusiasm for the Lord and His people.

7. Rev. Benny Hinn, a devout man of God, filled with the Holy Spirit and whom God has used and continues to use mightily throughout the world.

8. Zig Ziglar, the most highly recognized motivational speaker in the world, and to whom I am most likely related.

9. Rev. Joyce Meyers, an inspirational wise woman of God, who never leaves any stone unturned to help us all grow in the Lord.

10. Rev. Walker Epps, Superintendent of the United Methodist Church, Dothan, Alabama, well respected for his wisdom and compassion.

FOREWORD

Over 350 passages in the Bible pertain to fear, the most crippling disease on the face of this earth. Television and newspapers are the best tools Satan has with which to daily program fear into the minds of people.

Faith is the total opposite of fear. Actually, fear is perverted faith, for fear can bring to us exactly what we fear, just as it did to Job in the Bible. *Job 3:25* says, *"What thou has greatly feared has come upon thee."* The energy created by verbal acknowledgement of all the horrible things going on in this world today, primarily via television and newspapers, only serves to make the forces of evil even greater, and Satan rejoices as people become more and more afraid. Our subconscious minds are extremely susceptible to what is being programmed into them, even more so in the first hour after waking and the last hour before going to sleep. Most people wake up to the morning news and go to bed after the nightly news, starting and ending the day with negatives.

I urge you to be very careful of what you allow into your subconscious mind. Negativism breeds fear and doubt, and fear can cause a person to never want to leave his home. Fear brings illness and disease to people. Understand right now that your happiness lies in learning to manage your greatest asset, yourself, and your brain which is more powerful than any made-made computer and is your greatest tool. If you feed garbage in, garbage will come out. In order to have the ammunition to conquer Satan and to go out into the world with confidence, we should feed our minds daily with the Living Word of God. We can then create a wonderful life for ourselves and for others. *Proverbs 10:24* tells us, *"The fear of the wicked, it shall come upon him: but the desire of the righteous shall be granted."*

We are reminded in *2 Timothy 1:7, "For God hath not given us the spirit of fear: but of power, and of love, and of a sound mind."*

CONTENTS

OUTLINE
Fear Not: You Have Favor With God

I
Who Do You Think You Are?

Chapter One reflects upon my early life, my parents' struggles, and my relationship to my parents. It reveals many of the basic issues I believe that caused me to struggle in my personal relationships. It speaks about the reality of generational sin and how these cycles can be broken only through a personal and intimate relationship with Jesus. It describes my experience of receiving the baptism of the Holy Spirit in October of 1987 and how I began to grow in Christ. My thirty years in, primarily, direct sales is discussed, as well as the choices I made leading up to the necessity to apply for Social Security disability.

II

Anger – Mask of Fear

This chapter investigates some of the reasons people experience so much anger and some ways to deal with and work through that anger. The chapter outlines the wonderful benefits that we can experience by learning how to develop a personal relationship with the Lord and how to apply the Living Word of God to our lives. It also addresses proper nutrition, a necessity for proper brain function. Discussion of demon possession, the five steps leading up to it, and the weapons that God makes available to us to use in our battles are also included in this chapter.

III

You Can't Run From God

All of us have been guilty of attempting to fill the void in our lives in many ways other than Christ. Drugs, alcohol, and material possessions are just a few of the ways that come to mind. Chapter three tells us that, since God created us for His glory and pleasure, there is no way to run from Him. The only way to real freedom is through complete surrender to God through Jesus Christ. This chapter also relates how the Holy Spirit leads us and teaches us, as well as the necessity to transform our minds in order to look at ourselves and others through God's eyes.

IV

Entering Into God's Kingdom

God loves us just as we are right now, no matter where we are, what we have done, or what we will ever do. However, He desires a close, intimate relationship with us, and there are certain stipulations that we must follow in order to be able to walk closely with Him every day. Chapter Four reveals why we all need a Divine Power outside ourselves in order to work toward a more Christ-like nature. We cannot intellectually know God. He is spirit and must be worshipped in spirit. Jesus is The Way, The Truth, and The Life, and we must learn to humble ourselves as little children before God, or He will do it for us. We all need Christ-esteem instead of self-esteem. The only way to the true and eternal riches of life is to dethrone self and put Christ back on the throne.

V

The Spirit is Strong

Chapter Five discusses the five basic drives that we all have and they either push us into the arms of a loving Father, or drive us into a living hell, so to speak. There is, of course, a real and eternal hell. This chapter touches on the fear of uncertainty, which relates to every concern that people could possibly have involving health problems, unsaved loved ones, and the rapidity of the disasters occurring in the world today. People need to understand that we are spirit, mind, and body, and all of them must be fed in order to have balance in our lives. Feeding our spirits and our minds with the Living Word of God is the only thing that will break the yokes of bondage. There are facts in this natural world; however, God's truth, His Living Word, will override any so-called facts. We can learn to praise Him in the middle of a crisis and watch Him take a set of circumstances that the devil meant to destroy us with and turn them completely around for His glory. Forgiveness, which is not an option, is also addressed here. Loving others is not a suggestion; it is a commandment. Only by learning to fully embrace God's love are we truly able to look behind other people's anger and begin to love them into the Kingdom of God.

VI

The Power of Your Words

This chapter explains how God created the world with His spoken word, how The Word became flesh (Jesus) and came to dwell among us, and how powerful our words are, especially when we speak God's Word under the anointing of the Holy Spirit. We have all created the set of circumstances in which we presently find ourselves, and it began with our words. In order to change those circumstances, we first must learn to change our vocabulary. There truly is death and life in the power of our tongue. God's Word will never return unto Him void, but it will accomplish that to which it is sent forth; therefore, we all need to learn how to align our words with the Word of God and to speak those life-giving words into our circumstances. God told us to talk to the mountain (the problem) and to command it in the name of Jesus to be removed. Only born-again, spirit-filled people have been given this authority and are not afraid to use it against the evil forces.

VII
Prayer and Spiritual Warfare

Chapter Seven tells how our battles are first won in the spiritual realm before results are manifested on the physical plane. It describes different types of prayer and tells about the authority God has given us as born-again believers to command evil spirits to leave our lives or the lives of others for whom we are praying. This chapter also discusses how we wrestle against principalities and powers in high places and what we can do to break the strongholds in our lives to become totally free of all bondage. The supernatural power of Almighty God can be accessed, and people can become brave, fearless, praising warriors. This is what God wants from us.

VIII
Spiritual Gifts From God

The essence of Chapter Eight deals with the spiritual gifts outlined in *1 Corinthians 12:8-10*. God is willing to give these gifts to those who are ready to receive them. The gifts are the Word of Wisdom, the Word of Knowledge, the Discerning of Spirits, Healing, the Working of Miracles, Faith, Prophecy, Speaking in Tongues, and Interpretation of Tongues. The challenge lies in our level of faith and our own desire to receive them. In this chapter, I reveal the negative aspects of my health, why I believe I went through this phase of my life, and why I expect a complete healing of my mind, body, soul, and spirit. According to our faith, it is done unto us. We all operate at different levels of faith. My God is able to do exceedingly and abundantly above all I, or you, could ever ask.

IX

Harvest Time

Harvest time talks about Israel, a nation for over fifty years now, and the Jubilee in which we are living. This is a time when all things return to God as outlined in *Leviticus 25*; everything that can be shaken is being shaken in this world today, and people are coming to God by the thousands. The harvest is plentiful, but the laborers are few. It is a time when the wealth of the wicked is being transferred into the hands of the righteous, because God knows that they will use that money to help usher in the second coming of Christ. This chapter talks about tithing and how that money already belongs to God, and how we cannot outgive God, no matter how hard we try. He always takes what we give and multiplies it back to us as He blesses others through us. Through all these circumstances, including being challenged with serious health issues, I have grown closer to God than I have ever been, and I have learned to trust Him to a degree that I never dreamed possible. God has taken the hurtful circumstances of my life and turned them around for His glory and pleasure. Healing can be supernaturally spontaneous, or it can be a process while God still uses us in the interim, bringing us into wholeness. An in-depth discussion of fasting and the benefits derived from fasting are included here.

X

You Are More Than a Conqueror

Chapter Ten lists eight names of God, what they mean, and how God is free to manifest Himself to us in what He is when we praise Him. Praise is our primary weapon against Satan. Satan is real. He roams to and fro looking for those he can destroy; God is looking for those He can bless. The Holy Spirit is always gently nudging us, but He never forces Himself upon us. This chapter lists fifteen roadblocks that Satan uses against people to keep them from stretching their faith to reach for higher goals. When we learn how to control the good things in life (only with Christ living in our heart) rather than always riding on the coattails of other people's thoughts or actions, will we begin to enjoy the most exciting journey upon which we could ever embark. How we see ourselves determines how we live and what we accomplish. An engram is a lasting memory of an incident that occurred in the past. These are embedded deeply into our subconscious minds, affecting our present lives. Only God's grace and a close walk with Christ will enable us to learn how to become more than a conqueror. The battle was won 2000 years ago. If you are a born-again believer, then you are, or should be, fighting the good fight of faith from a position of victory. I pray these universal truths of God will strengthen you and help you to press on towards the mark for the prize of the high calling of Christ Jesus because you truly are more than a conqueror through Christ Who loves you.

Last Section

In this section of my book, I share a few poems and songs that the good Lord has given me thus far on my journey.

Chapter One

Who Do You Think You Are?

O n August 3, 1945, Ocie Ziglar Crockett gave birth to her fifth daughter, Glenda Gayle Ziglar. Yes, that is my God-given name at birth. Born in a little southern town called Dothan, Alabama, I had no brothers. I was supposed to have been a boy; at least that it what my parents told me, and on more than one occasion, I might add. The doctor knew how badly they wanted a boy after having four girls, and he thought that I was a boy. What can I say? Here I am, maybe still tomboyish in some ways, but nevertheless I am a woman.

As I look back now, there were several factors that highly contributed to my emotional instability. With my parents wanting a boy so badly and letting me know that, I surely must have felt, to say the least, somewhat unwanted. In addition to that, I do not remember my Daddy ever holding me in his arms or telling me he loved me. On many occasions, just sitting around on the front porch and talking to friends, neighbors, and relatives, Daddy would sometimes say, "Kids are meant to be seen and not heard." I know what you are thinking. If she is a Christian, she should have forgiven her father by now, and I have. Forgiveness is what Christianity is all about. The point is this – we all need to be very careful what we say to our children. Discipline, along with an abundance of love and praise, are necessary ingredients if children are to grow to be emotionally healthy, law-abiding citizens.

Generational sin and inherited ignorance are very real. We learn much from our parents who mean well, most of the time, but due to the lack of education they received when they were growing up, it is quite easy for low self-esteem to become the fruit of children who never receive parental encouragement. Therefore, unless the cycle can be broken, a downward spiral trend develops. In order for this cycle to be broken, someone has to receive the baptism of the Holy Spirit. The Bible says that if you have the Holy Spirit, you have no need that any man teach you anything. He, the Holy Spirit, will lead you into all Truth.

My Mother and Daddy had to struggle for as long as I can remember. Having received only a ninth grade education, Daddy was a carpenter. He never allowed Mother to work, except at Christmas time. She worked in one of the local department stores downtown. Mother insisted on working during Christmas so that she would have enough money to buy Christmas presents for me and all my sisters and their families. Some people would probably say we were poor, but I never felt poor. I saw many other families who seemed a lot worse off than me. Daddy had built most of the apartments and houses where I grew up, and we rented them out. Many times my sisters and I would take some of the neighborhood children, put them in the tub, and bathe them. Their parents hardly recognized them.

My parents did love me. Mother was always babysitting for her grandchildren so that I could continue high school and get my diploma; otherwise, I would have had to quit school at the age of fifteen and get a job. When I was sixteen, Daddy bought me a 1950 black Ford. He had let me start driving his pickup truck when I was twelve. I used to load up all the neighborhood friends and go round and round the block. I remember one occasion when we were coming around the corner a little too fast. Daddy was sitting on the front porch watching, and as we turned the corner, we slipped into a big ditch. Thank the good Lord above that I knew to bear down on the gas to come out of that ditch. Daddy would have been really mad if he had needed to call someone to pull that truck out of a ditch. Thank you, Jesus.

As far as spanking goes, I remember Daddy spanking me only twice in my whole life, but that was quite enough. I was about twelve when I got the first one. We were living upstairs and Daddy and Mother had a laundromat downstairs. Daddy and Mother and I were sitting on the screened porch one night. I was just listening to them talk, and Daddy was complaining about one of my sisters coming over so late to do her laundry. I went straight down to the laundromat and delivered this bit of news to two of my sisters and their husbands who were all down there talking. Needless to say, it was the wrong thing to do. That should have taught me a lot about gossip right then. That big, wide leather belt left blue marks on my legs; today, someone would have screamed child abuse.

I was about thirteen when Daddy spanked me the second time. I was head over heels crazy about a boy who lived about a block away. Daddy and Mother sometimes would go to Sneads Fish Camp down in Sneads, Florida on the weekend. This particular weekend they happened to come back earlier than I had expected them to, and I had the house key with me. I went to the movies with Danny. We watched the movie twice, and then we walked home. We were about halfway home when I saw my Daddy coming in his old, blue truck that had his name written in big, white letters on the side. He pulled over to the curb, got out, grabbed me by the arm, and quickly put me in that truck. He let me know in no uncertain terms that he did not like that boy having his arm on my shoulder. Thank God I had a bunch of petticoats under my dress; that spanking was not as bad as it could have been.

Those two spankings were quite enough for me. Daddy put the fear of the wrath of God in me, and I knew I had better walk a chalk line from then on, and I pretty much did. My friends thought I was a little Miss goody-two-shoes in high school, but I knew better than to step out of line. Unlike them, I had a Daddy who would jerk a knot in me.

Yes, I have forgiven Daddy for all the hurt, mostly emotional, that he caused me. Unfortunately, it was only after he died in 1986 that I was able to do so. On the flight home from Atlanta to attend his funeral, I wrote Daddy a poem, and I asked the Lord to help me read it at his graveside funeral. I was glad I had put my arms around Daddy and told him that I loved him when I saw him crying after my sister's seven-year-old son drowned. I had seen my Daddy cry only one other time, and that was when his father died. Daddy sure did love little Scotty; he took him everywhere he went.

Scotty's death was a nightmare for my family and one we will never forget.

Scotty and his dad had gone fishing at Fort Gaines, Georgia, on a Friday night with another man and his ten-year-old son. They had anchored the boat up close to the dam. When the horn blew to let the fishermen know that the water would be let through the dam, Rudolph, my brother-in-law, and the other man couldn't get the anchor out of the water. It was hung, and the boat overturned. None of them had on life jackets. The two adults and the other boy made it out of the water. Scotty was nowhere to be seen. They searched and searched, but they found no trace of Scotty. Scuba divers came in from Panama City, Florida, and searched unsuccessfully for three days. They finally dragged the river, and the hook caught Scotty in the jaw. He had turned blue by the time they brought him up.

I was in my twenties when Scotty drowned. I had spent a lot of time babysitting that little fellow when he was smaller, so it was a very sad time for me and everyone in the family. A friend that Scotty went skating with on Friday nights sent him a flower arrangement in the shape of a bootskate. Another friend knew that he loved to fish, so he sent flowers in the shape of a fish. During the funeral, Scotty's Mother, my sister, Shirley, called out his name over and over. It was a very emotional time. Mother told us before they even found Scotty that he had talked to her on the Thursday before about going to Heaven, so we know he has a very special place up there with our Lord and Savior, Jesus Christ.

Another event that happened in my life unfortunately impacted my life in a very negative way. When I was 13 I was molested by a family member. I never told anyone. I was too scared. It was many years later when I was directly asked by a family member if this had ever happened to me that I was brave enough to tell. I guess I didn't want to cause a major emotional confrontation at the time. So, needless to say when you take a girl who has never heard their father say, "I love you," coupled with being molested by a family member, and add the emotional devastation of your first love and husband leaving you for a gay guy, what else but total rebellion could be the outcome? I became very bitter towards men. This started a pattern in my life that has certainly been very difficult to overcome, to say the least. I have forgiven all those who have deeply hurt me, though it hasn't been easy. Unfortunately I went through more than one failed marriage because I didn't love myself enough. I was so far away from God for many years, and I attracted to me, men who also had emotional problems. Only by staying close to the Lord have

I been able to forgive. Actually it is Jesus in me Who does the forgiving; because on our own its impossible.

During my junior and senior years of high school, I went to school in the mornings and worked as a nurse's aide at a local hospital in the evenings. I wanted so much to be a nurse. After I graduated in 1963, I knew my parents couldn't afford to send me to nursing school, and I did not have enough self-esteem to realize that if I wanted it badly enough, I could have worked my way through. I took only one year of typing in high school. It seemed no one in town wanted to hire someone fresh out of high school. I accepted a job with Warner Brothers packing women's undergarments, and that lasted only three days. It didn't take me long at all to find out that working in a factory was not for me. May God bless all the people who do work in them. I left Dothan, and went to New Orleans to live with my oldest sister, Jeanette, and she helped me get a job with Southern Bell Telephone Company as a long-distance operator. I was not happy there either, because I had to work a lot of split shifts and late at night, and the chief operators would stand over my shoulder, constantly watching every move I made. They could plug into my position at any time and listen to me. I ended up moving to New Bern, North Carolina, and marrying my high school sweetheart. He was in the Marine Corp at the time. Our son,

Paris, was born in 1965. His father named him after a Trojan prince from Greek mythology. After we were married about 4 ½ years, he left me for a gay English professor. I was devastated. After my divorce, I became very bitter towards men and developed a rebellious attitude towards society in general. I fooled around with drugs and alcohol, trying to escape the emotional pain. For three months I would take speed to get out of bed in the morning and Valium to go to sleep at night.

Then I married a second time. Three months later he was killed. Two years later another guy came along and rescued me from sin city, or so I thought, and we moved from Atlanta to Boca Raton, Florida. We lived there about a year and then moved to San Diego, California, because his sister was living in Borrego Springs, California, with her husband and two children. My second son, Brent, was born in 1974. Of course I always wanted to blame my husbands for everything that went wrong, but in reality, we seem to be like magnets, and attract the people who reflect some of our own inadequacies and innermost problems. There is no excuse in this world for some things I did, at least not one good enough, and you can believe I have suffered through many years of guilt, tears, and deep sorrow. Praise God I have been forgiven and have finally forgiven myself. Because of fear for my life and having no one to turn to, since I was living two thousand miles from home, I left Brent, my ten-month-old son at the time, with his father and came back home to Alabama. My decision-making abilities left much to be desired. I loved my son; if I had not wanted him, I would not have waited over nine years to have him. He was so precious. We listened to a lot of music, and he would be on his hands and knees and would rock back and forth to the music. He loved music then, and he still does. As a matter of fact, he composes guitar instrumentals. I am so thankful that Paris took the initiative in 1993 to find Brent. I am also very thankful that Brent has a gentle, loving, forgiving spirit. Brent came to Dothan to visit us for a couple of weeks in 1996. I become overwhelmed with emotions when I think about that first encounter with Brent at the airport. I have so much for which to be thankful, especially where my two sons are concerned. I thank God that He hears our prayers. I can promise you that God hears a Mother who is down on her knees crying out to Him for her children. Pleading the blood of Jesus over them daily and reading Psalms 91 is invaluable, too. We are all in a spiritual battle, whether we recognize it or not. The devil roams to and fro seeking whom he can destroy, but God also goes back and forth seeking people upon whom He can shower down His blessings. I recognize the subtle tactics of the enemy, and he will not win. I read the end of the book.

Only Jesus Christ can fill a person with the kind of love it takes for a child to say, "Mother, I forgive you for abandoning me." Only with Jesus Christ living inside me am I able to admit that I did such a horrible thing (to the whole world).

After a long period of being single, I married again in 1983. Instead of encouraging me to do something with my own God-given talents, Daddy had always told me I should marry an insurance man. He thought they made lots of money. This husband was not an insurance salesman. However, I turned him into one, at least temporarily. He was never happy selling insurance, but he was very good at it. In fact, after we both became managers for Globe Life Insurance Company; we were given a rare opportunity. Before I tell you about that, let me share this with you. We were in Bowling Green, Kentucky, working as managers, making good money, and spending all of it. We bought a new brick home (new to me, since I had never had one). Our manager was all excited about going to a *Born to Win* seminar presented by Zig Ziglar. Ricky was so excited that it rubbed off on me, and I was walking on cloud nine, too. It had been a month or so since we had buried my Daddy. I had brought his Bible home and had been reading it every day, studying diligently about this thing called faith. My husband went on a weekend hunting trip with Ricky, our branch manager. That Friday night I went into my bedroom, turned off the lights, and lay down on the bed. Now, for you nonbelievers, I would just like to say God bless you. The room was pitch black, and as I looked over to the right, there in midair was a waterfall about one foot in width and about four feet high. I heard an audible voice quote *John 7:38: "Out of your belly shall flow rivers of Living Water."* It was as though the image was electrified, and the water was actually flowing. It startled me, and I jumped up and turned on the lights. I calmed down enough to lay back down. I said, "Lord, that sounds like something for preachers." He said, "Just trust Me." In *John 4: 13* God says, *"If you drink of the water I am offering you, you will never thirst again."* God also told me not to be afraid and that He would always be with me. I was just beginning to trust Him.

Shortly after that, we moved back home to Buford, Georgia. My husband was growing quite weary of selling insurance. Being a manager and continually trying to produce enough sales to please someone else, especially when you don't enjoy it, is very stressful.

Randall Baskin, the owner and founder of Continental Life Insurance Company in Nashville, Tennessee, believed in us so much that he gave us an exclusive contract for the whole state of Georgia on a Medicare supplement that would pay 100% of all that Medicare would not pay. In addition to that, he paid our office rent and all of our bills for one year, as well as giving us all the furniture for the office. All we had to do was to visit all the other agencies throughout Georgia and give them a contract under us. They, in turn, would have all of their agents selling the policies. Well, we blew it. I tried for many years to blame my husband for our failure. In reality, though, we were both to blame. However, we did manage to sell enough group medical insurance for Time Insurance Company to qualify for a trip to Costa Del Sol, Spain and Tangiers, Africa. That was quite an experience. Anyway, the more I studied all those motivational books, the more I realized that the common denominator was faith. I began to analyze the idea of selling someone a product based on fear. God began to show me that fear was the opposite of faith. To me, at that time, having insurance began to seem like betting on a negative, and that bothered me tremendously. I have come to terms with that now, however. My husband had executiveitis. He wanted to sit with his feet propped up on his desk half the time. He just simply was not happy selling insurance. I have finally learned that we can only change ourselves.

In October of 1987 I had a profound experience with the Lord, which has dramatically altered the course of my life, to say the least. Thank God that He is in the people-changing business. This happened after a bout of depression and confusion that spanned over many months. On Friday I had been out in the rural areas of Buford, Georgia, just north of Atlanta, trying to make myself knock on some doors to try to sell a Medicare supplement policy. I could not do it. I just drove aimlessly and finally came home in total despair and with feelings of worthlessness. After taking a long, hard look back at my life, I sank lower into depression, and thoughts of suicide began to filter into my mind. I pulled in the driveway and just sat there for a long time. I finally pulled myself together and went to the bookstore and bought another motivational book. This helped only temporarily. I went to church on Sunday as usual. Before I go any further, let me back up and say that God had been wooing my heart for about a year or so. After Daddy died, I told my sisters that all I wanted was his Bible.

Daddy had been living by himself for several years. Mother left Daddy after fifty years of marriage, having had no choice. He started getting violent, and he would throw lamps and other things. I think Daddy had some health issues that adversely affected his behavior; Mother had no choice but to leave. Daddy never went to church with the rest of us when I was growing up, but he would listen to preachers on the radio and read his Bible. He once told me that he had read the Bible my sisters had given him all the way through several times, so I knew it meant a lot to him. I know he missed my Mother, even though he never really treated her very well; he was always saying things to put her down. I know now that Daddy did the best he could, and I have heard that his Mother was extremely hard and cruel. You see how such treatment is handed down from generation to generation. People need the Lord so much, and they don't even know it. Most people don't realize that the void in their hearts can be filled only with Jesus. That's just the way that God created us.

Another way I had of learning to forgive my Daddy was by writing a song entitled *Daddy's Bible*. I wore out that old Bible learning about faith. Now back to that Sunday afternoon when I had my mountain-moving experience with the Lord. After lunch, I closed myself off in the back bedroom. I was miserable; I had all these feelings welling up inside me and no one to talk to, so I broke down crying, and as I did, I found myself asking Jesus to come into my heart and wash me from my sins and set me free. I cried and cried and cried. There are really no words that can explain how I felt, but I'll try. It was as if God just engulfed me with the warmest feelings one could ever imagine, and I have never felt so much love. It was incredible. It was like liquid love. In fact, it was a miracle. When anyone receives the baptism of the Holy Spirit, it is indeed a miracle. It is also a miracle when a person is born again. I was born again when I was twelve, but, as you now know, I was a backslider in a big way. This was the most beautiful experience I have ever known. The peace I felt cannot be described by mere words.

I read a book entitled *What You Say is What You Get,* which is based on the Bible. I literally felt like God had just handed me a blank check. I started to put into practice what the author, Charles Capps, was saying, and it worked. Let me tell you what I mean by that. We had just hired a new girl to sell insurance, and I knew I would be the one to train her the next day. The rest of the day after I put that book down, I went around saying, "Thank you, Lord for a $1,000 Medicare supplement sale." I wanted to impress our new saleslady on her first day out in the field, so I woke up raring to go like Zig had taught me to do. Susan and I drove out into the country, up around Braselton, Georgia. We knocked on five doors and talked to a few people. We didn't see any potential for a sale anywhere, but my faith was still intact. After all, if faith worked for the author of that book, then it would work for me, too. I believed it! Let me say that again; I believed it!!! This is key to everything. *Matthew 9:29* states, *According to your faith be it done unto you."* When we came to the sixth house, the lady came to the door, we introduced ourselves, and we went in and started to discuss insurance with her. She had a fairly good policy, but it was coming up for renewal soon and ours was better coverage. To make a long story short, not only did we write her up, but she took us down the road to her sister's house, and we wrote her up, too. This was $1,800 worth of insurance, and I was working under a 55% contract. Do you think this impressed Susan? I should say so, but not for long, because she didn't work with us for long. She never could overcome her fear of knocking on strangers' doors.

It was not easy trying to share my new enthusiasm for Christ with my husband and his family. When people have an experience like this, they want to tell everyone, because they want others to have the same freedom they have found. It is extremely difficult to keep it to yourself, in fact, impossible. Many people accept Christ into their heart without having such an experience, just as I did when I was twelve and invited Jesus into my heart. However, being baptized in the Holy Spirit is entirely different. Even after an experience such as this, it doesn't mean that you are perfect now. God just gives you an entirely new heart with which you begin to see more from His point of view. You are filled with more grace and peace which enables you to handle difficult situations much more maturely and confidently. You are able to walk in victory more often, because you are learning to stretch your faith, and you begin to see that faith is what God honors. He absolutely loves the attention, and He rightfully deserves it. After all, He created you and me and everything, didn't He? Of course He did. Do I believe in the big bang theory? Yes I do! According to *Genesis 1: 3,* God said, *Let there be light,"* and bang, there it was. God actually spoke this world into being.

Immediately after an experience such as this, Satan always comes around and tries to make you think that you are just too emotional and that nothing is any different. Sometimes people fall back into some of their old patterns quite easily. It happened with me; I ended up getting another divorce.

I moved to Dunwoody, Georgia, a suburb of Atlanta, to be close to my best friend, Phyllis, and started selling carpet. This was a salesperson's Utopia. We were furnished with four to five appointments a day, six days a week and were taught how to do a one call close on what was sometimes a whole houseful of carpet. We sold 6.2 billion dollars worth of carpet in 1989. We worked very long hours all over Atlanta and in all the surrounding little towns within fifty miles of Atlanta. My first appointment was around 10:00 A.M., and I would usually get home around 10:00 or 11:00 P.M. Most women would never think about being out there alone and going all over the place, never knowing where they would be next. Sometimes we had to drive for an hour or more just to get to an appointment.

I was making good money, and the Lord had been dealing with me about tithing. I remember how nervous I was when I first stepped out in faith and wrote a tithing check for $50.00. I stayed very close to the Lord, talking to Him all day long as I drove between appointments. After four days, I received a lead for carpet at a management company. They managed two large homes for mentally and physically impaired people, and both homes needed carpet. I gave my presentation, went and measured the two homes, came back, gave them the price, and I walked out of there with a $12,000 sale, which meant over $600.00 to me. God blessed me with this sale after I stepped out in faith and took Him at His Word. *Malachi 3: 10* says, *"Bring ye all the tithes into the storehouse, that there may be meat in Mine house, and prove Me now herewith, saith the Lord of Hosts, if I will not open you the windows of heaven, and pour you out a blessing, that there shall not be room enough to receive it."* Verse eleven promises, *and I will rebuke the devourer for your sakes, and he shall not destroy the fruits of your ground."* What an awesome promise! I had always given sporadically to the church, a dollar here, five dollars there, maybe ten dollars on a rare occasion. This is the only place in the Bible where God tells us to prove Him. We serve a wonderful and awesome God Who is worthy to be praised, not just because He can and will do wonderful things for us, but because He already has. He loves us so much that He sent His Son to die on the cross for our sins. What a price to pay to show someone how much you love them!

I trained a lot of salespeople and received overrides on them for awhile. When the owners refused to pay me any more overrides, I hired a telemarketer and started my own carpet business out of my apartment. I took this program to Nashville, Tennessee, and set it up with three telemarketers out of the basement of my cousin's house. We did okay; we broke even for the three months that we worked the program. However, I think we went in there at the wrong time of the year.

Before I left to go to Nashville, I was attending Mt. Paran Church of God in Atlanta and absolutely loved listening to Dr. Paul Walker, the pastor. The church had a huge lay ministry. Seeking God for direction, I had prayed and prayed, and I thought that I was being led into the lay ministry. I knew that God was in the process of giving me a great deal of compassion for other people. I went to the head psychologist at Mt. Paran and answered 150 questions. I then attended a one-day seminar with about twenty other people. We were paired off so that we could practice the procedures we were being taught. Afterwards, the speaker presented a scenario and asked what we would do. She said, "Suppose a very troubled man comes to your office. After being there a few minutes, he tells you that he has a gun, and he just might as well blow you and himself away." The speaker then asked what we would do; no one said anything. The Lord had been dealing with me about fear for several months, so I spoke up and said what God said: *"Perfect love cast away the fear."* I said I believed that no matter what the guy may be saying, God had created him with a heart and obviously had been dealing with him, or he would not be there seeking help. Therefore, if I stayed focused on the Lord, then He would help me work through that situation by ministering to the man in such a way as to bring him into the full grace of

God. The speaker was startled at my answer. Another thing that bothered me was that under Georgia law, and I'm sure in any state, if someone came in and told you that they had molested someone, then you would have to report it to the authorities. I had a major problem with that. Here they were in church, in counseling, seeking God strongly, baring their souls to you, and you had no option but to turn them in to the authorities. It took me several years to understand why they have to do that. The truth is, just because God forgives us for something does not mean that there is no restitution to pay. We all are accountable to man-made laws as well as God's laws. Our justice system may not be perfect, but it is the only one we have; if we think some things are unfair, then we should get active and try to bring about change instead of complaining about it and doing nothing.

I had been digging, praying, and writing - writing, playing and digging, learning to forgive. To be honest with one's self is a very cleansing and freeing experience. I read one of Benny Hinn's books titled *Good Morning Holy Spirit*. I prayed for God to reveal to me everything I needed to deal with to get past the emotional pain. He did. I had heard a psychologist on TV say to make a list of all the people who had hurt you and all of your sins. Sounded easy enough. I went to my bedroom and sitting up in bed I proceeded to work on my list. This took far longer than I expected. Anyway, after I did that, as I pounded my fist into the pillow calling out each name, I would tell them I hated them. Then after I went through each name I went back and lifted them up to God and forgave each one and projected love to them. Working on my list of sins was much harder to do, but the only way to get rid of the guilt and shame is to acknowledge what we have done. God's Word says we are all as filthy rags without Jesus.

I kept praying and seeking God for real purpose and meaning for my life, and finally He revealed to me in a dream that I was to write this book. Praise God! I had purpose and meaning now. The spirit is strong, but the flesh is weak. I started writing, but my flesh did not have the discipline it needed to get much work done; that is why it has taken so long to complete the book. Also, little did I know that I had much more to learn about fear before God was ready for me to go forth with this book. I am not saying that I have learned all there is to know. If we ever feel like that, we may as well just lie down and die.

In 1992 I came back home to Dothan, Alabama. I wanted to be close to my family again, and Paris, my oldest son, had already moved back a few months before. Rhodes Furniture hired me to sell for them, and once again I stepped way out in faith believing that I could sell $30,000 worth of furniture per month, as well as a certain amount of add-ons, such as fabric protection, wood kits, etc. Over a period of eight months, I averaged $28,500 per month, with about $1,600 per month in add-ons. They used fear intimidation every month when they brought the salespeople into the manager's office for a review. Our jobs were constantly threatened. I truly believe that they hated to let me go. However, they had just hired this young man not long after I started, and they felt like they had to make an example out of me. I left there and went to work for Barrows Fine Furniture. It was wonderful not having quotas to meet. Therefore, with no pressure, we could focus on the customers' needs more and truly give them the service they deserved. I enjoyed the special orders and working with the customers selecting fabrics, coordinating all the styles of furniture, and assisting them in mixing fabric patterns. I had finally made it back home and found a new job; my life was in transition in more ways than one.

Sometimes physical and/or emotional problems can cause a person to become somewhat out of sync. I was at the age for my hormones to start giving me a fit, and they did. I hated the idea of taking prescription drugs, and I still do; I don't take any right now except for thyroid, Praise

God! However, I found myself spending a lot of time in my apartment watching Christian television and crying buckets of tears for all the starving children in the world. I knew this was not healthy. It was during this time that I became a prayer warrior. My nephew was beaten by five guys who jumped on him, and he almost lost his life. *James 5: 16* tells us that *the fervent prayers of a righteous man availeth much.* Praise God for that promise. I cried and prayed and cried and prayed some more. The doctors said it was a miracle that he lived. You must understand that I don't claim to be righteous on my own. It is only because Jesus lives inside of me. It is Christ in me and Christ in you that is the hope of glory. Not too long after this happened, I made the mistake of going to a club with one of my sisters. I had not been in a club in years. I decided that I was spending too much time in my apartment crying; I needed more balance in my life. Can you guess what I did next? That's right; I got married again.

Everything in me told me that I should not marry him. He was involved in a very sticky situation with the law, and I felt very deep compassion for him. He claimed to be innocent, and I chose to believe him. He was extremely persistent. I tried harder than I have ever tried in my life to make this marriage work. This was the only church wedding I had ever had, but the odds were stacked against us from the very beginning.

About twenty years prior to our marriage, he had been a minister of music in his church, and he still attended church sometimes, so I kept telling myself that this marriage would work. There was just no way that God would allow me to make another wrong decision where marriage was concerned. The lawsuit against my husband was like a black cloud hanging over our marriage, and it consumed most of our conversations. To make matters worse, his home church tried to throw him out. They had tried this twenty years before as well. The first time involved fundraisers that the church held to purchase new carpet. My husband had found a good price on some carpet, so he took it upon himself to order it. Some of the members rebelled. The membership might be compared to the Hatfields and the McCoys. The bickering between members dated back thirty years or more.

My husband and I had been in a board meeting, and in my opinion, the pastor had handled himself very inappropriately. He verbally jumped on my husband and threatened to call the police in response to something he had said. The pastor should have talked with my husband privately in his office instead of threatening him in front of others. They were both strong, assertive individuals whose personalities clashed. In addition to that, the pastor knew about the lawsuit against my husband, and he just automatically tuned in to fear. After the board meeting, the pastor went to most of the church members in their homes stirring up discord. He called a meeting to attempt to get him thrown out of church.

The pastor, having visited the members on the "Hatfield" side of the church, stood up in front on their side of the church, sowing discord with his words. Discord is one of the seven sins that God says He hates most. He spoke for ten minutes trying to get them to admit to the negative things that they had told him about my husband. They sat there in silence. Those on the "McCoy" side of the church were the members who had known my husband for many years and liked him. After the pastor spoke, the superintendent asked if anyone else wanted to say anything, so I went up front. I addressed the pastor. I turned toward him as he sat in the front pew and asked him how he could take it upon himself to be the judge, the jury, and God. He hung his head. I spoke a few more minutes. I knew that my husband was not perfect, but he really did not deserve all this. The situation had gotten way out of hand. This man was my husband, and if I did not stand up for him, who would? The pastor joined me up front and halfway apologized to him. The meeting adjourned shortly after that. It was not very long after this ordeal that the members voted the pastor out of the church. I never dreamed that I would be in a situation like that. I believe it is called refiner's fire. Gold is purified in the fire; I don't believe I am a solid gold bar yet, but God isn't through with me.

I left my husband in August of 1996 and moved in with my then eighty-eight-year-old Mother. She had just lost her husband, my stepfather. I have discovered that if you have Jesus, you really have all you need. Jesus is enough for me. He is everything I need. He gives me love and unspeakable joy, and He brings me peace that passes all understanding. His grace is sufficient for me, and that grace helps me to rise above any and all adversity. He wipes away my tears and removes all my fears. He is giving me wisdom and discipline over my flesh. He has given me a heart that longs to reach out to other hurting people and help bring them into the Kingdom of God. He supplies all my needs. I have everything I need right now, but I know that God has a much better plan for my life. I am learning to receive that plan now, and I praise God for using me as an instrument of His love.

In 1962 and 1963 I had worked at the hospital as a nurse's aid for half a day each day after attending school for the first half of the day. I absolutely loved it. One of the head nurses even let me give shots. I wanted to go to nursing school, but as I mentioned before, I lacked the self-esteem and I got married instead. I feel there is nothing sadder than to look back over one's life and realize so many regrets. Because of this, in April of 1997 I accepted a job as a nurse's assistant in a nursing home. I knew it would be hard work, but I had no idea just how hard. The affiliated hospital would reimburse my tuition after a year's employment to attend nursing school. In addition, they would give in-house transfers. Even though I was over qualified for the position, I accepted it. I had no idea that the wing they put me on was made up of mostly totally dependent residents. I loved working there in one respect, though, because I could look in their eyes and tell them that Jesus loved them and see the sparkle. I could also pray with them and for them. Being in a position to do this on the job meant the world to me. Unfortunately, the physical work load was much more than I could bare. I didn't realize then that one of my 30 year old silicone implants had ruptured in the Spring of 1996 and each time I would lift a resident, over 40 neurotoxins were flooding my body, including formaldehyde, epoxy glue, and epoxy hardener. In October, 1997, I suffered a ruptured, herniated disk in my lower back from lifting the residents all day long. It wasn't until February, 1998, that workmen's comp paid for me to have back surgery. All of this contributed to my having developed two different disorders of the muscles. I was diagnosed with fibromyalgia, which is biochemically induced. I also developed myofascial pain syndrome, which has to do with physics in relation to the mechanics of the body. The muscles are in a fight or flight syndrome at all times, and all the body circadians are thrown off. This produces a wide range of problems, pain, mental confusion, and insomnia. The pain is in the muscles and, although it is not acute, it is chronic and can vary from hour to hour, or even minute to minute. The sad thing is that millions of people are suffering from these problems, and unfortunately, doctors receive very little formal education relating to the muscles or to nutrition. Chiropractic adjustments helped a little. Acupuncture and massages helped somewhat. Everything I have read or been told says that fibromyalgia cannot be cured. However, let me interject here that I know the Great Physician. The Holy Spirit has re-confirmed to me just how crucial and vital all the B vitamins are, not only to the proper functioning of the brain, but also to the muscles. People with fibromyalgia are known to be deficient of thiamine, one of the B vitamins. Oftentimes for some reason our bodies do not absorb these very well, so we have to take more than what the average healthy person would take. I have found that by taking a B100 complex three times a day along with extra thiamine, and B12 the pain in my muscles decreased. Another very important thing to mention here is that I discovered sugar depletes the body of all the B vitamins. The average American diet consists of approximately 140 pounds of sugar per year. Sugar is, by far, one of the worst things we can put into our bodies. Our brain needs B vitamins to function properly; otherwise the neurotransmitters do not work properly, causing loss of memory, foggy feelings, and disorientation. The muscles need the B vitamins. A deficiency of vitamin B results in pain. In fact, it is interesting to note that Alzheimers patients have a very low level of vitamin B12. Look at all the people on Prozac. If they all had an extensive vitamin analysis done of their blood, I feel certain they would all show deficiencies of the B vitamins. I am thoroughly convinced that with proper nutrition and detoxification the body can heal itself, because God designed it that way in His infinite wisdom. I don't know how long it will take for my body to be in perfect balance again, but I praise God that He has brought me a long way since October of 1997. He has shown me exactly what to do every step of the way along my journey in seeking to be made perfectly whole. We serve a mighty awesome God.

Everything that I have shared with you about my life thus far has brought us to where I am now, sitting in front of my computer and finally writing the book that God instructed me to write several years ago. I have worked on it from time to time, but I never had the discipline before that was needed. Events happen in God's own timing, though. I know that God told me to write this book; it was very plain in a dream I had. The book had a gray cover on it and the words "Fear Not" in huge, bold, white letters.

Who do I think I am? I am a follower of Jesus Christ, who loves Him more than life itself. I just happen to be, at this particular time, serving as Pastor of Tabernacle United Methodist Church in Hartford, Alabama, as well as Pastor of Pleasant Ridge United Methodist Church in Enterprise, Alabama. I had to pass a lot of psychological tests and go through all the steps in the Candidacy Program in order to have the honor of pastoring these precious people in these two little country churches. I am so excited about what God has done and continues to do in my life as I learn to yield totally to the Holy Spirit to lead and guide me. Who do I think I am? I AM A KING'S KID!! Jesus Christ is Lord of Lords and King of Kings. In *John 6: 4* He said, *"I am The Way, The Truth, and The Life, and no man cometh unto the Father except by Me."* Jesus lives in my heart and if you let Him live in yours you can overcome anything.

Chapter Two

Anger – the Mask of Fear

I don't know who *they* are, but *they* say we are born into this world with only two fears: the fear of falling and the fear of loud noises. If this is true, then all the rest of our fears that we carry around have been learned. As children, we learn by trial and error to be afraid of certain things. For instance, touching a hot stove will cause physical pain and injury; therefore, we learn to a certain degree to fear hot things. Of course, this is a healthy fear. We must learn to use common sense and to be careful. Unfortunately, society has a way of instilling many, many fears into our minds as we go through life. Well-meaning parents, teachers, friends, neighbors, relatives, and yes, sometimes even pastors do this unconsciously. Actually, most of the fears we accumulate while growing up and through our early adult years are unwarranted. Eighty-five percent of our worries never even happen. Worry is really just paying advance interest on trouble before it comes due. In *Matthew 6: 34* Jesus said, *"Take no anxious thought of the morrow:...Sufficient is the evil in this day."*

I touched briefly in the previous chapter on a child's need to experience emotional love from both parents in order to grow up emotionally healthy. If we don't get those demonstrations of love as we are growing up, we will be constantly looking for love in all the wrong places. It is very important, especially for a little girl, to receive demonstrations of love from her Mother and even more important to receive this same kind of love from her father. If she doesn't, the chances are far greater of her establishing a pattern of running from one relationship to another. Because we attract basically the same type of people we are inside, a girl's expectations are unlikely to be met in such a case. Many wrong choices are made under these circumstances, and deep-seated anger begins to develop, along with feelings that life has given her a rotten deal. We learn that by shouting or pouting that we can get some attention, even though it is the wrong kind of attention. We rationalize that it's better than none. In a marital relationship, it takes an extremely mature person (one who received the proper emotional love and discipline while growing up or one who has done a lot of soul searching and learned self-discipline and self-control) to be able to come even somewhat close to understanding the sudden outbursts of anger coming from a spouse. The overly assertive, domineering, and controlling person is many times repressing deep-seated feelings of anger and self-pity. They continually blame other people, either quietly or sometimes openly, for all their problems. These are the people who need love the most. Only with Jesus living inside us are we able to look beyond the anger and see them as God sees them. People must be loved into the Kingdom of God. Jesus said, *"I have come, not to condemn the world, but through Me, the world might be saved."* However, we must be emotionally secure within ourselves to truly love others with agape love (God's love).

There are many reasons why some people carry around so much anger. They could have been molested as children or abused in some other way. Yes, people who are hurting need to see Jesus in us. They need to know that we love them unconditionally. That does not mean that you have to make yourself a doormat. These people need to be constantly pointed to Jesus. He is the Savior, not you and me. However, they need to see us consistently revealing the power of the Lord as we daily exhibit grace, joy, love, and peace because these are the same virtues they want. These wonderful gifts can be obtained for a lifetime here on Earth but for an eternity through developing an ongoing relationship with our Lord and Savior, Jesus Christ.

Now don't get me wrong. It is quite normal to get angry from time to time and to express that anger. It must have an outlet. That energy must be released, but it needs to have a healthy way of releasing itself. Getting angry every other day and screaming and shouting is not normal or natural and is certainly not the way God intended us to live here on Earth. If a person is frequently hostile and exhibits sudden outbursts of anger, severe mood swings, depression, lack of motivation, or problems with drug or alcohol abuse, then that person should definitely seek professional counseling. A Christian counselor would be ideal in this case. You can be sure that such a person is struggling inwardly with many fears and doubts concerning relationships, self-worth, work, and life in general. This person is primarily afraid of the whole process of life and is afraid to trust anyone, including self and God. Such people have usually been verbally or physically abused or neglected, and in many cases, they have been through several relationships that have not worked out. As they go through life, they pile one resentment on top of another because they were not taught as children how to give or express love or how to communicate their feelings properly. As they become more bitter and more angry, they learn to like themselves less and less. They look for ways to escape from reality through drugs, alcohol, etc. They are resisting the need to look within themselves first in order to change the way they see things. Perception and attitude are everything. Some people think we are born into this world as precious, innocent children who learn to be bad. This isn't true. The Bible says that we are born into this world in sin with a sin nature. That means we have a tendency to sin because we live in a fleshly body. God sent His Son to die on the cross because He loves us, and He knew that our own strength would not enable us to overcome all the problems we would face without a Savior. In God's awesome and infinite wisdom He knew we would need Jesus living on the inside of us to help us overcome the desires of the flesh and all the rest of the problems we face every day.

We can never change the way we are until we understand *why* we are the way we are. People need to take a long, hard look inside themselves and be totally honest with themselves. This is called soul searching. Our souls are made up of our wills, our minds, and our emotions. Saying cruel things to others or constantly blaming others for everything only produces layers of guilt. If we are angry all the time, it is usually because we have not forgiven someone in our past, whether it be our parents or anyone else. To resist the need to grow and mature is to begin to rot and decay, with sickness, poverty, and death just around the corner. Hostile outbursts caused by anger usually push the people we love further away from us, and life is a self-fulfilling prophecy. Here's what goes on in a hostile person's mind: "I knew I couldn't trust him. He is just like all the rest. He doesn't really love me; if he did, he wouldn't do this or that. I don't need him. I can make it on my own." What this person is really saying is, "I don't feel worthy of love." People with this attitude don't know how to give or to receive love. They have not matured enough to even want to compromise with their partner. Things are going to be exactly the way they want them to be, or they are not going to be at all. I believe the key issue here is balance. God wants balance in all things, relationships as well as the environment. Indeed, fear will bring to you exactly what you fear.

Nutrition can also affect one's emotions. Please understand that if our bodies do not get the proper nutrients through vitamins and minerals, then we cannot expect it to function properly. This includes our brains. Lack of proper nutrition can cause a chemical imbalance in the brain. Through many studies, science has begun to prove that many people who are diagnosed, or maybe I should say labeled, with such disorders as bipolar and those who supposedly have Alzheimer's disease, are actually suffering from a Vitamin B complex deficiency, primarily B12. Vitamins and minerals must be taken into the body in the right balance. Unfortunately, the Earth has been depleted of most of its natural nutrients because of acid rain and problems with the ozone breaking down. According to *Leviticus 25*, we were supposed to have tilled the land for six years and then let it rest on the seventh allowing it to replenish itself. We haven't done that. We have worked the land unceasingly. It seems parasites and bacteria are running rampant in today's society; therefore, it is more necessary than ever to take your own health into your own hands. The saddest thing in the world to me is to know we have a brain, which is far greater than any man-made computer, and not to learn how the brain functions and what is takes to make it function properly. There are four key amino acids that the brain must have to function properly: tyrosine, glutamine, cysteine, and phenylalanine. These are vital to brain function. Tyrosine helps you to handle environmental stress and phenylalanine keeps you from being depressed. Glutamine enhances the brain's reaction time. These are precursors to neurotransmitters which shoot messages to the brain. Imbalances of the chemicals in the brain can cause a person to constantly be in a fight or flight syndrome. We are not born with Prozac or Zoloft in the brain, or any other anti-depressant for that matter, so these drugs are not the answer. There is no need to put synthetic chemicals into our bodies, which sometimes make things worse. However, if you are on such a prescribed drug, *please do not stop taking it abruptly; this could be detrimental.* Sometimes it is necessary to take certain drugs for a period of time. Go to a health food store and find a complex multivitamin with a wide range of minerals, enzymes, and amino acids. Enzymes are necessary to balance all the chemicals in the brain. Note: Enzymes in food are totally destroyed by heat (cooking). Then slowly taper off the prescribed drugs. I suggest you talk this over with your doctor first. I am not a doctor, nor do I claim to be. However, I encourage you to study. You ought to become You, Inc., always seeking God through Jesus Christ. The Holy Spirit will lead you if you only ask. If your brain and your body are not operating to their fullest potential, then how can you ever expect to live life to the fullest and realize the plan that God has for your life? Yes, improper behavior can be, and in many cases is, directly related to improper nutrition. Doesn't this make sense to you?

We must begin to realize that there is no one on Earth who will ever meet all of our expectations because we are all human beings. We are not perfect. We all are operating at different levels of awareness, and the level of awareness that each of us operates on is in direct proportion to the amount of truth that we are willing to admit to ourselves about ourselves. We cannot force anyone else to operate at our own level of faith because we are all unique individuals made up of our own thoughts and experiences in life. We all perceive things differently to varying degrees. Understand that! No one is all right or all wrong. No one is all good or all bad. We are just operating at different levels of consciousness at times. However, what God wants is for us to learn to see ourselves and others the way He sees us. Our feelings about things are always changing. God never changes. He is the same yesterday, today, and tomorrow. He loves us. Sure He always meets all our needs, but He wants to do more than that. He wants to shower us with blessings, but He is a very jealous God. A close, personal relationship must be developed with Him. When we are in a pleasant and morally right situation with another person, and we are operating on the same level, then things are clicking, and progress is being made. This is where we get the old saying "two heads are better than one." The Bible says in *Matthew 18: 19," If any two people on earth can agree on any one things, they shall have whatsoever they shall ask."* Sometimes you can pray and pray about something, and nothing happens until you find someone to pray with you and come into agreement with you. There is much power here.

Learn to forgive! Get on with life! Learn to say you're sorry when you know in your heart you have hurt someone. It won't kill you. In fact, you will feel good about yourself. Ego and pride can create a very lonely, cold-hearted person who lives a miserable life. It's your choice. We always have choices. Whether they be good or bad choices, they will reap good or bad circumstances. Are you choosing to tune your thoughts in to the evil forces stirring up strife, anger, worry, hostility, fears and doubts, jealousy of affections, or of other people's money, or are you centering your thoughts on God's love? You can acknowledge the chaotic situations of this world while still standing on the promises of God, believing that He loves you no matter what you have done. If God be for us, then who can be against us? I am truly convinced that lack of money, lack of inner peace, sickness, and many other negative things are only a lack of understanding about how to apply the Living Word of God in one's life. Taking the time to learn how to apply God's Living Word will give you:

1. Peace that passes all understanding
2. High self-esteem and confidence

3. Faith to rise above adverse situations

4. Love of all mankind

5. A sincere desire to reach out to help others become all they can become

6. The wisdom to make your dreams come true here on earth.

We must understand that what we center our minds on will multiply. There are laws of cause and effect. I consciously choose to center my mind on Almighty God and to trust totally in Him and in the process of life, looking for the good in other people. Perfect love casteth away the fear (*1 John 4: 18*). Here again, the choice is up to each individual. Which do you choose? Are you a part of the problem or the solution? Do you tune in to fears and doubts concerning everything – anger, lustful thoughts, words, or actions, or are you a good finder who encourages and helps other people to learn to love themselves by teaching them how to fully embrace the love of the Lord? It usually takes having a broken spirit and being in a state of total despair and loneliness before a person can accept Christ and invite Him into his heart. One cannot just intellectually accept Christ. His peace and His love must be expressed through the emotions of the heart. The Bible says there will come a day when every knee shall bow and every tongue confess that Jesus is their personal Lord and Savior (*Philippians 2: 10*). However, how precious that salvation is to those that are saved is strictly up to the individual. Many people accept Christ, but they immediately let the devil talk them into believing that nothing is any different and do nothing to pursue an extended relationship with Jesus. People need other people to help guide them, teach them, and encourage them. Unless we are constantly pursuing a close relationship with Jesus, then we are slipping backwards. There are no ifs, and, or buts about this. *Romans 6: 11* tells us, *"Likewise reckon ye also yourselves to be dead indeed unto sin, but alive unto God through Jesus Christ our Lord."* When a person accepts Christ, he needs to realize that he is a new creature in Christ and has been set free. However, there are still choices to make every day. Each person who accepts Christ must make the conscious decision to work with the Holy Spirit every day in order to stay on the path of righteousness and in the perfect will of God. If we do not put the Lord first every day, then we are not in the perfect will of God. Wisdom is the principle thing; *Proverbs 4: 7* states, *"therefore get wisdom: and with all thy getting get understanding."* When we stumble and fall, God is always right there to pick us up. He never gives up on us. Sin opens the door to Satan to rush right in and cause mental, emotional, physical, or financial problems. We sometimes experience all of these problems. We must learn to be quick to repent and slow to anger as God instructs us in His Word.

We must realize that most of our parents did the best that they knew how to do with whatever education they had. Education in this sense does not necessarily refer to book learning in school; it refers to morals and the love of God. Most of our parents raised us as well as they were capable of doing at the time. Have you ever thought that maybe they didn't get enough love when they were growing up? Give them a break! Grow up! Let go of the past! It has no value to you! It will only hurt you! Don't let the sun go down on your wrath! If you are in a relationship now, you are going to have problems. They are inevitable, and they are necessary for growing and maturing. These are the times when we grow the closest to the Lord. Sit down and talk about your problems. Learn to communicate. Compromise! Work it out! Get on the same wave length in pursuing your dreams. Work together toward common goals, not against each other. Dreams can come true, but it's up to you. There are three types of people in this world – people who make things happen, people who watch things happen, and people who wonder what happened. Which type are you? Adopt this little saying from Dr. Schuller: "If it is to be, it's up to me!!"

Psalms 37: 8 tells us to *"Cease from anger, and forsake wrath: fret not thyself in any wise to do evil."* Unless anger is dealt with, it can give an open foothold to Satan. A person can actually become demon-possessed. There are five steps that these people go through before they become totally possessed and under the compete control of foreign and evil forces*:

1. Regression – a loss of hunger for God
2. Suppression – a loss of joy; anger has not been dealt with
3. Depression – a loss of strength
4. Oppression – the stage where a person is full of guilt
5. Obsession – the stage where a person believes one thing from which he cannot escape

All five stages have to do with the mind. The next stage is possession, which has to do with the spirit, and it is when a person comes under complete and total control of foreign, evil forces. The Holy Spirit will leave a person at this point. However, there are weapons that can be used to help this person overcome. Unfortunately, at this stage, one usually cannot fight the battle alone. It requires other people who love and care about this person to use the weapons that God has made available. These weapons are as follows:

(*Benny Hinn)

1. Prayer – This must be fueled by the Word of God. The Bible says in *2 Corinthians 10: 4, "For the weapons of our warfare are not carnal, but mighty through God to the pulling down of strongholds."*

2. Praise – This gives energy to prayer. Start praising God, and He will do wonders. The devil is crippled when you praise God. *Psalms 149: 6-8* says, *"Let the high praises of God be in their mouth, and a two-edged sword in their hand; to execute vengeance upon the heathen, and punishments upon the people; to bind their kings with chains and their nobles with fetters of iron."*

3. Speak the Word – *Revelation 12: 11* tells us, *"And they overcame him by the blood of the Lamb, and by the word of their testimony; and they loved not their lives unto the death."*

Let the redeemed of the Lord say so!!

Numbers 14: 28 promises, *"As truly as I live, saith the Lord, as ye have spoken in Mine ears, so will I do to you."*

You must claim what you want from God! You must take your hands off the situation! You must send the angels to minister for you! God said that His people perish for lack of knowledge. Sometimes people have the knowledge but don't take the time to draw near to God or to learn how to apply the knowledge to their lives and the lives of their loved ones. The truth is, we have not because we ask not. There is no problem too big for God. He knows everything, and He is in everything. He just wants us to acknowledge Him and the fact that He has ultimate control over everything; He wants us to trust in Him. We must learn to walk by faith, not by sight, and we must learn to stretch our faith. You *can* learn how to control your emotions. You can learn how to maturely respond to other people and not to react to something they may have said or done that rubs you the wrong way. How we respond to other people determines the degree of our success in achieving joy, peace, love, and grace, along with a lifestyle that is pleasant and fulfilling.

You never have to stay in discouragement if you will always remember these three things as you turn to God for help and pray this way:

1. Father, You know my situation and feel my discouragement. I believe you are here with me going through this with me now.

2. Father, You are in control and I surrender to Your perfect will. I cast all my cares unto You because You said You will never leave me nor forsake me.

3. And, Father, I believe You are taking this situation I am presently in and turning it completely around and You are blessing me because You know I will give You the glory and honor. In Jesus' name, Amen.

Chapter Three

You Can't Run From God

I n all God's magnificent glory and divine plan for all
our lives, He created us with an inborn desire to grow
closer and closer to Him. He created us for His pleasure, not
ours, to praise Him, to honor Him, and to give Him credit for
being in total control of everything. Even down to the most
proclaimed atheist, God searches the hearts of all people in
the silence of the night as they lay their heads down on their
pillows to go to sleep. Deep down in the hearts of all human
beings, they acknowledge our heavenly Father, though they
may deny Him in the presence of other people. How sad it is.

In 1987, shortly after I rededicated my life to Jesus, I
started teaching Sunday School to my own peer group. This
was in a small Methodist church in Buford, Georgia. One
day our minister was visiting in our home, and I asked him

why he thought more people didn't turn to God. I personally had just experienced so many wonderful benefits, such as peace that passes all understanding, joy, vitality, enthusiasm, and just a renewed sense of overall well-being. I couldn't understand why so many people tended to put God on a shelf and take Him down as needed (I was certainly one of those people for many years). The Holy Spirit revealed the answer to me the next day in a book I was reading based on the Bible. The most difficult thing for a just and honorable person to do is to accept something (God's saving grace, a gift from God) for which he doesn't feel worthy. This is where the paradox comes in. We are all sinners, and we do come short of the glory of God. However, it is my opinion that this has been drilled into the subconscious minds of many people to the point that they actually feel so much shame and guilt that they are reluctant to turn to Jesus. I had listened to Satan for so many years telling me that the Bible was something that a bunch of people had gotten together many years ago and written in order to keep from having chaos in the world. During the three day mountain moving conversion experience, the Holy Spirit woke me up a five o'clock one morning and sent me the words to a poem entitled *The Truth*. Jesus said in *John 8: 32, "And ye shall know the truth and the truth shall make you free."* My friend, I am here to tell you that when I invited Jesus into my heart, confessed my sins, asked for forgiveness, and asked Him to cleanse me and make me whole, all doubts concerning the Lord were totally removed. I was filled with His Holy Spirit and I can promise you that He is alive. I am also beginning to understand why people call the Bible "the Living Word of God." It truly is. When we speak the Word, it is as though Jesus lives in the ethers of this universe. His Spirit does. Nothing brings Him on the scene any quicker than when you speak the Word or just whisper His name. There is tremendous power in His name. Don't ever forget that. Nothing puts Satan to flight any quicker than quoting the Word of God out loud. Satan hates it. God loves it.

A person can accept Jesus as personal Lord and Savior and not receive the full emersion of the Holy Spirit. However, one can ask God to fill him with the Holy Spirit, and that's when the pure and perfect love of God Almighty comes to reside in the heart of that person. Old desires and things you used to love to do no longer satisfy you as God begins to give new desires and interests. Old things pass away; all things become new. When we are filled with the Holy Spirit, we are filled with a deep, compassionate love of all mankind and a sincere, deep desire to help other people develop a close relationship with the Lord. God's Word says in *1 John*

2: 27, "After ye receive the Holy Spirit, ye have no need that any man teach you anything. The Holy Spirit will lead you and teach you." This is a very rich and friendly universe. God is in control of everything. He has given us freedom of choice, of course. Unfortunately, when Adam and Eve were living, Eve made the wrong choice when she listened to the voice of Satan telling her to go ahead and eat the apple from the tree of knowledge from which she would gain all the knowledge of God. She disobeyed God by doing so, thus giving birth to the fight for mankind to conquer the powers of darkness (Satan). Satan wants to destroy people with fears, doubts, lust, anger, hate, hostility, violence, and greed. As born-again Christians, God still gives us choices. We can choose to go on living in our own will, putting the dollar first and foremost in our thoughts while hoping and praying for a better life and better circumstances, and this can be done. However, this is not a satisfying life. Only Jesus can fill the void in a person's heart. I am finding it is far more rewarding in every way to keep my priorities right. We cannot worship God and mammon, and the first and greatest commandment, according to *Matthew 22: 37* is, *"Thou shalt love the Lord thy God with all thy heart, and with all thy mind."*

Now don't get me wrong. There is nothing at all wrong with money. We all need it, and God wants us to have it.

There is certainly no virtue in poverty. Money is not evil. The love of money is a sin; specifically, the Bible says in *1 Timothy 6: 10, "For the love of money is the root of all evil."* Money is actually just a form of energy. God wants us to have financial abundance and to live prosperously. We can certainly do a lot more with money than we can without it. If we become financially independent, we can help a lot more people who truly need help. Jesus said in *John 10:10, "I am come that they might have life, and that they might have it more abundantly."* At any rate, even as born-again Christians filled with the Holy Spirit, we still have choices. We can tune the frequencies in our brains to the spirit of deceit, or we can learn to tap into the wonderful and magnificent power of God Almighty by daily prayer and praise and by applying the Living Word of God in our daily lives. This is the only way to develop monumental, mountain-moving faith, the kind that helps you to take control over Satan, who tries to destroy us with fears, the most crippling disease on the face of this earth.

You can move from city to city and from state to state and from spouse to spouse, but you cannot run from God. He knows everything about you, and He is always right there with you whether you acknowledge Him or not. He created all and He is in all. He created us for His pleasure and He is always wooing our hearts toward Him. When we are struggling to live our lives in our own wills, it is indeed a continual struggle, and our lives tend to be filled with anxiety. To experience God's peace (that which passes all understanding) is to experience peace of the soul which is made up of mind, will, and emotions. To do so, we must first make a commitment to: 1) spend time alone with the Lord everyday; 2) spend time reading God's Word everyday which breaks the yoke of bondage; 3) spend time in prayer and worship, asking God to reveal His plan for our lives to us. Yes, God has a plan for each and every life. He said, *"I know the plans I have for you, plans to prosper you, not to harm you." Matthew 6: 33* says, *"But seek ye first the kingdom of God, and His righteousness; and all things shall be added unto you."* Well, to me this means that we would never want for anything. He said all things, didn't He? This is a promise to all God's children whom He has redeemed from the curse of the law because they have been made joint heirs with Jesus by accepting Him into their hearts.

It is true that most people think becoming a Christian means being perfect. This is very far from the truth. Just because a person has been born again and received the Holy Spirit does not mean he will never do anything wrong ever again. Lightness and darkness both exist. Satan is the ruler of the darkness. Darkness is represented by anger, fear, hostility, depression, confusion, jealousy, envy, and self-pity. Even though light dispels darkness, even the most devout Christian slips out of the light sometimes because people are influenced from time to time by the imperfections of this world, our environment, television with all its violence and negativism, and other well-meaning people. Yes, we all stumble and fall because we are human beings. However, when we react to another person with anger or unkindness, then the Holy Spirit will convict us in our hearts, causing guilt until we repent of our sin. We must always be quick to repent and quick to forgive if we want to get ourselves in a position to experience all the blessings God has in store for us. We must always watch everything that goes into our minds and take control of our thoughts. We cannot stop the evil thoughts that sometimes come to us, but we can command them in the name of Jesus to leave us. Resist the devil, and he will flee from you. If we are continually replaying negative situations in our minds or allowing negative comments from others or from ourselves to be fed into our "inner ear," then we are blocking the flow of God's blessings. In this case, your inner ear refers to what you hear with deep down inside your heart. Your body is a temple of the Holy Spirit. This includes your mind.

The heart is fed through the mind, and out of the heart comes the issues of life. *Luke 6:45* tells us that *"Out of the abundance of the heart, the mouth speaks."* Negativism will drain your spirit and feed you full of fear. We must condition ourselves, either out loud or silently, through positive self-talk of God's loving words. Out loud is really better. We can also teach ourselves how to link our thoughts to pictures (creative visualization). These tools are powerful, but they must be used for the good of all people concerned. Then you will be provided with more blessings than you can possibly imagine. *Romans 12: 2* reminds us to *"Be ye not conformed to this world, but be ye transformed by the renewing of your mind."* *Proverbs 4:7* tells us that *"Wisdom is the principle thing, therefore get wisdom."* Have you ever wondered why there are so many subliminal tapes on the market today? People are earning millions of dollars from them, and nothing is wrong with that as long as they are giving God credit, giving back to God to help spread the Gospel, and living in the will of God by being obedient to Him. However, there are many people out there today who understand the basic principles of God and the universal laws of God, but they are not giving God credit. Unfortunately, they are leading many people astray. In my opinion, the New Age movement best represents this fact. Universal laws of God work just as

81

surely as the laws of physics or gravity. However, applying these laws simply to achieve more and more material possessions cannot and will never satisfy the human spirit. God did not create us that way. *Deuteronomy 8: 18* says, *"Thou shalt remember Jehovah, thy God, for it is God Who has given us the power to get wealth."* Yes, these laws are workable and applicable even to the non-believer, but those people who leave Jesus out of the picture will never be truly happy and fulfilled. I cannot stress enough that things do not satisfy. ONLY JESUS CAN FILL THE VOID IN THE HUMAN HEART. There may be those of you who do not agree, but I have come to the conclusion, after walking closely with the Lord for several years and reading and studying the Bible and books based on the Bible, that the subconscious mind is a direct link to God. People need to understand how powerful their thoughts and words are. As Dr. Paul Walker, pastor of Mt. Paran Church of God in Atlanta so eloquently put it in one of his services, "Whatever the mind thinks, the mouth speaks, whatever the mouth speaks, the brain records, and whatever the brain records, the body manifests."

Since childhood, we have all been programmed negatively to one degree or another. We all suffer emotional problems to one degree or another. However, people could save themselves a lot of time, effort, energy, and years of therapy if they would just make the decision to accept the truth that God's psychology is far greater than any man-made psychology. Don't get me wrong; modern psychology has its place in our society, but it is not the complete answer. Whatever the question, Jesus is the answer. Only with Him living in our hearts will we ever be able to overcome all the adversities in this world or to forgive our parents or ourselves. We do not have the power in our own strength. All the strength and power belong to a divine presence outside ourselves, the Holy Spirit. He is available to us upon request. He will never force Himself on you. When children misbehave, they need discipline as well as love. They should be instructed that they are being disciplined for their bad behavior, and they should be assured that they are still loved even though it was necessary to discipline them. Also, when a child is constantly told that he can't do something, he grows up with an "I can't helpless attitude." If he gets into more serious trouble as a teenager and the parents tell him how horrible and no good he is, then the whole family tends to treat him as an outcast. He is jokingly called the black sheep of the family. This child will and does suffer years of emotional turmoil and pain inside and easily gets caught up in a pattern of bad behavior, thus creating a track record of making wrong choices involving drugs, alcohol, and perhaps even crime, simply because his/her self-esteem was not at the level it should have been. They were programmed negatively. Like it or not, we are all a direct result of, primarily, parental guidance. They say we have developed our basic character and personality by the age of five. In order to grow up to be normal, healthy, mature people, we need a tremendous amount of emotional love from our parents. If we are abused mentally with negative mental programming, physically through molestation or uncontrollable beatings, or emotionally by a lack of demonstrations of love such as hugs and words of love, then of course we do not grow up healthy with a sense of self-esteem. Unless we truly love ourselves, we find it almost impossible to give love to others or to receive love from others when we are older because we don't feel worthy. The morals of this country must revert to the old-fashioned morals. These are learned from Christ. Only Jesus, as He instructed in *Philippians 4:8,* can help us to keep our minds focused on what-so-ever things are pure and lovely.

Many famous and successful people throughout history have discovered the power of the subconscious mind. The well-known author, Robert Louis Stevenson, would make direct commands to his subconscious mind just before drifting off to sleep. We all have a wonderful tool available to us, our brains. Why don't we learn more about our brain? The reason is because we can't see it or touch it. We know we have one, but people tend to take it for granted. I know just about everyone, before drifting off to sleep, has said to themselves, "I have to get up at a certain time in the morning," and invariably you wake up at that certain time or maybe within five minutes or so of that time. Now doesn't that alone warrant learning more about the human brain and how we can get it to work more effectively for us? I have discovered this tool, and it is the primary reason you are reading this book right now. *Proverbs 3: 5-6* says, *"Trust in the Lord with all your heart, lean not unto your own understanding. Acknowledge Him in all your ways, and He will direct your paths."*

As I mentioned before, at one time I thought God was leading me to go into the counseling ministry. I knew that I had been given a tremendous amount of love for other people and that there had to be an outlet for that love. I began to pray really hard about this matter. I began to lean on God more and more and to seek Him daily for His will. This did not happen easily, but finally He revealed to me that I was to write this book. It was a gray book with large, white letters on the front that said, "Fear Not." This was not revealed to me until I made a direct request to God just before drifting off to sleep. If we make known to God our requests in the receptive state of mind, requests that are pure and good and will help other people, then answers can come in a flash the next day, in a dream, or perhaps through other people. The spirits of darkness can also enter dreams. You will know whether or not your dream came from God, for God is love. In *1 Kings 3: 5* we read that *"the Lord appeared in a dream to Solomon by night, and said, Ask what I shall give thee."* No, you can't run from God, but why should you? Why would you even want to when He loves you more than anything in this world?

Chapter Four

Entering Into God's Kingdom

*J*ohn 3: 3 warns, *"Lest ye be born again ye cannot enter into the Kingdom of God."* God truly loves each and every human being just as they are right now, no matter where they are, what they are doing, or even what they have done in the past. However, God wants us to be all that we can be. He has a perfect plan for each and every person, but we have to learn to listen to His voice, trust totally in Him, and praise Him continually (not literally, but what I mean is to develop consciousness).

God knew that in giving us freedom of choice that we would make many wrong choices by trying to live in our own will and keeping God on the shelf. In making the wrong choices, we have suffered mental, physical, and emotional pain, shame, and guilt. However, in His perfect plan for our lives, He created a way out for us. *John 3: 16* states, *"For God so loved the world that He gave His only begotten Son, that whosoever believeth in Him should not perish, but have everlasting life."* He sent Jesus, His only Son, to die on the cross for our sins. He knew there would be many people who would feel like they had come to the end of their rope and like they had made the wrong choices in life. He knew that people would need a Savior to love them and to give them strength and courage once again. However, there was a catch to it; they had to ask. They had to humble themselves before Him and let Him know how much they loved Him and needed Him. Yes, Jesus has already paid the price for our sins. To think otherwise would be to call God a liar, wouldn't it? Therefore, I urge you right here and now, if you have never acknowledged Him as your Lord and Savior, to lay this book aside for a few minutes. Quietly kneel down on your knees and start talking to Him. Ask Him to come into your heart and to carry all your burdens for you. Let Him know that you truly and sincerely repent of all your sins and that you cannot carry around all the guilt and shame any more. Just simply acknowledge Jesus as your Lord and Savior, and you will never be the same again. You will begin to see things in such a different light. You will experience blessings every time you turn around. You might say, "Well,

I just can't give this up, or I can't give that up." Not many people can give up things they have enjoyed for many years in their own strength. It requires a strength outside ourselves to be able to do that. He does not say, "Zap, you are perfect." He just begins to replace some of your old ways with new and fresh ideas and interests. There was only one perfect person, and that was Jesus. Jesus can and will empower you with strength beyond your imagination to be able to overcome the evils of this world as you learn how to discern certain spirits. Growing and maturing is a long, slow process. May we never cease to learn and to grow. When we think we have learned everything there is to learn, we begin to decay, and then death is just around the corner. In fact, sometimes we learn that we have to constantly relearn many things we learned a long time ago.

Matthew 13: 11 tells us, *"It is given unto you to know the mysteries of the kingdom of heaven..."* We are all in a continual state of transformation, hopefully learning, growing, maturing, and changing our ways and our values because God created us with an inborn desire to grow closer to Him and to become more like Jesus, more patient, more kind, and more loving toward others. We do become either bitter or better. In God's eyes no one is more important than anyone else. We are all His children, and He loves us all the same.

Some of us are a little more intimate with Him because we have drawn near to Him, and He in turn has drawn near to us. God does not have any favorites, but He does have lots of intimates, and these are the believers. God wants us to have a peaceful, beautiful life here on Earth and forevermore. He wants us to love Him and to trust Him totally. However, we cannot become one of His intimates and receive all the wonderful things He has in store for each of us unless we accept Jesus into our hearts. *Matthew 18: 3* says, *"Except ye come as little children ye cannot enter into the kingdom of heaven."* One can never know the true joy of living without accepting Him, confessing Him as Lord and Savior, and choosing to believe in Him. There will always be a void in the heart of a person who refuses to accept Christ, and that person will always be trying to fill that void with other means such as food, alcohol, drugs, lust, and/or money.

One cannot know Jesus and learn to trust totally in God through the intellectual mind. May God bless all the people who are studying theology today and in the future. Some pastors are truly called by God. Then again, some have chosen to be a pastor as a profession and have never received the baptism of the Holy Spirit. Entering into God's Kingdom, which must be done by accepting Jesus, must be done in and through the emotions. Usually a person is in a state of despair, with no hope at all for the future, before he/she invites Jesus into their heart. The Bible is written in a code. Without the love and belief of Jesus in our hearts, we can read it until we are blue in the face, but we can never truly understand it. It is as though the word has a protective covering around it like a shell that can't be cracked open. Once a person is filled with the Holy Spirit the messages in the Bible come alive as the Holy Spirit reveals them to us. Thus comes the saying "the Living Word of God." I am here to tell you that the Word of God is powerful. It is meant to be used against Satan and to help you to overcome all your fears and doubts. God's Word brings you peace, prosperity, and good health, and it helps you learn how to let God's love shine in and through you so that other people's lives are touched, helping to bring them out from under the powers of darkness. Praise God for His perfect plan of salvation through Jesus Christ!! Jesus reveals His plan for us in the *sixth chapter of John* several times:

John 6: 35: "I am the bread of life; he that cometh to me shall never hunger; and he that believeth on me shall never thirst."

John 6:44: "No man can come to Me, except the Father which hath sent me draw him..."

John 6: 51: "I am the living bread which came down from heaven: if any man eat of this bread, he shall live for ever and the bread that I will give is My flesh, which I will give for the life of the world."

Satan, however, has other plans for us. He wants to continually replay bad memories in people's minds. This is how he destroys people. Jesus said in *Luke 9: 62, "No man, having put his hand to the plough, and looking back, is fit for the kingdom of God."* However, Jesus also reminds us in *Luke 9: 56* that *"the Son of man is not come to destroy men's lives, but to save them."* Satan's plan for destruction begins in the mind when we experience feelings of not being loved, rejection, unworthiness, self-pity, shame, guilt, confusion of all kinds, indecision, depression, or thoughts of suicide. We must learn to control our thoughts in order to control our lives. When we concentrate on the problem, it always gets worse. Feelings change, so why not learn to change them quickly? Don't hold on to self-pity or discouragement. It is time wasted. No one person can ever measure up to all of their own expectations, no matter how hard that person may think they are trying. Learn to quickly forgive and get on with a productive life. Forgiveness is what it's all about. We cannot forgive anyone in our own strength; it is not in our human nature. We need help to do this. We cannot get off a self-destructive course on our own. We need a power outside ourselves. We need Jesus. There are too many instances which accumulate over a period of many years that cause our hearts so much pain and sorrow. We get caught up in a downward spiral, destructive course, some moving more rapidly than others, unless we choose to change courses. No one can force another person to do this; each person must do so on his own. However, we can pray for others and help bring them quicker into the light. Jesus said in *John 3: 3, "Except a man be born again, he cannot see the kingdom of God."* Jesus also tells us in *John 3: 5-6, "Except a man be born of water and of the Spirit, he cannot enter into the kingdom of God. That which is born of the flesh is flesh; and that which is born of the Spirit is spirit." John 3: 7-8* states, *"Marvel not that I said unto thee, Ye must be born again. The wind bloweth where it listeth, and thou hearest the sound thereof, but canst not tell whence it cometh, and whither it goeth: so is every one that is born of the Spirit."* God is a spirit, and He must be worshipped in spirit. He operates in you, through you, and for you to the extent that His Word is hidden in your heart, to the extent that you are willing to spend time alone with Him in prayer, and to the extent that you will openly worship Him while you are gathered together with others. He tells us not to forsake the gathering of ourselves together.

A spiritual awakening comes after a person is born again and has accepted Jesus into his heart. It is as though the blinders have been removed from the eyes of those who have accepted Jesus. Indeed they have because they begin to see things in a whole new perspective, and they are seeing things through God's eyes much more clearly than they ever had before. However, we must accept God's salvation through faith. *Ephesians 2: 8-9* plainly states, *"For by grace are ye saved through faith: and that not of yourselves: it is the gift of God: Not of works, lest any man should boast."* YOU MUST ACCEPT JESUS IN ORDER TO BE SAVED. When you do, you are aligning yourself in a position to receive abundant blessings from Almighty God, Who is called Jehovah Jireh, our God and our provider. This is only one of His magnificent names. God, as our provider, has abundant blessings in store for all who accept Him.

You are a unique human being. There is no one else on the face of this earth just like you. *Matthew 10: 30* tells us that even the hairs of your head are numbered. God knows everything about you and still loves you and has a wonderful plan for you, one full of love, joy, peace, and financial blessings. It is up to you to accept what He wants to give you.

Does the new birth mean that you will never have any bad feelings toward anyone? I'm afraid not, but we can come to a place where we recognize the subtle tricks of Satan. He is always trying to steal our joy by trying to make us dwell on little things that people have done that hurt us. Learning how to be slow to anger and quick to forgive is your major advantage in everything concerning you, not only in your health, but in everything you want to achieve. Whatever the question, love is the answer. Why? The answer is because God is love. It is in God that we live and move and have our being. God breathed the breath of life into every human being at birth. God is pure love, and in the depths of every human heart is His pure love. Underneath the pain, the anger, the greed, the lust, the revenge, the resentment, the jealousy, and the envy is God's pure and unconditional love just waiting to break through all the yokes of bondage that seek to destroy people. We are instructed in *1 Corinthians 16: 14* to *"Let all that you do be done in love,"* and *John 15: 17* says, *"These things I command you, that ye love one another."* Take heed of the word command. This obviously is not a suggestion. Every human being was created by God in His image with an inborn desire to give and to receive unconditional love. This is called agape love, the love of God. It is only when we are experiencing a desire to withhold love from someone (even though we may feel we have a right to) that the creative and powerful energy of love is blocked. It is then that the blessings of God cease to flow easily in and out of our lives. If we are right on the inside, then things will be right on the outside.

There are only two types of reasonable people. There are those who have already found God (actually He wasn't lost; we are or were) and are learning to trust in His perfect divine order of things, and those who are still searching for Him with all their heart but haven't found Him yet. They believe in God, *but* they have not yet experienced an intimate relationship with Him. They know *about* Him, but they don't really *know* Him. Some people are very caught up in the rat race of life. They are chasing the almighty dollar, beating their heads against the wall, or blaming everyone in the world for their particular set of circumstances. They sense that nothing short of a divine power outside themselves is going to help them learn to live life victoriously. This is God Almighty urging them to acknowledge Him as the eternal source of all good and wonderful blessings. God does not force Himself upon anyone, but He is always gently nudging people. *Isaiah 45: 23* says that there will come a day *"That every knee shall bow, every tongue confess that Jesus is Lord and Savior."*

We all need divine assistance to perfect our nature. Jesus is the same today as He was 2000 years ago. The Spirit of God, already on the inside of every human being, is likened unto being supercharged with God's warm, beautiful love and peace when a person accepts Jesus and is converted. Everyone has doubts before conversion, but once converted, they know that they know that they know. The Holy Spirit begins to reveal things to the newborn children of God. They begin to realize that the burden of all their sin, guilt, and shame is no longer weighing them down. They have been set free, praise God! They have been given the wonderful gift of God to begin again with a clean slate. At this point, most people have come to realize that their old ways were not working for them. They were not happy or even the least bit fulfilled in any way, at least not in a lasting way. These people have been given the desire to learn to love themselves and to love others. How highly prized this new birth is to each individual is the key to determining how closely that person will work with the Holy Spirit in learning how to become all that God wants him/her to be. It is not reasonable to think that all vices and desires of the flesh are instantly brought under control of the Spirit. New interests seem to crowd out the old, harmful habits and vices. We forgive others more easily. We start to gain much compassion for other people.

Many mysteries of the universe seem to start unraveling to us as we start applying the Word of God to our lives.

Having entered into a new spiritual dimension and experimenting with the universal laws of God, which are all in the Bible, one becomes aware that he or she is tapping into the supernatural power of God. It is very mystical and very exhilarating! This spiritual journey is one of the most fascinating and most interesting journeys one will ever encounter. Those who embrace this journey begin to realize that keeping their minds on the pure and lovely spiritual things and on God's universal laws, along with much love and adoration and praise to God, will result in God showering them with an abundance of love, grace, peace, harmony, success, and power to overcome. Everything falls into place just as quickly as we choose to believe it will. This is learning to trust in God. However, even a born-again Christian can have fears occasionally, but he/she quickly learns that they must turn their eyes back to God in prayers of praise, asking for guidance and release of their fears. *Ephesians 2: 4-6* assures us that God's love gives mercy, grace, life, and exalts, and *Ephesians 3: 19* tells us that love is an experience and a relationship. The powers of darkness cannot prevail in a home where the family daily turns their eyes and hearts up to our Heavenly Father in prayers of praise and thanksgiving, for there is much power in gratitude for what we already have. Unless we are thankful for what we already have, how can we expect God to give us anything else? God lives in the praises of His people. This is God's home address.

You can rest assured that whatever we are allowing to dwell in our minds will multiply itself in our own little natural world. If we are dwelling on a lack of money, we will be continually caught up in a state of lack. If we can learn to look at the world as a beautiful place in which to be, full of God's blessings with plenty to go around, forgive people daily who hurt us, ask for forgiveness daily (this is a necessary cleansing process), connect with others in the spirit of love, be thankful for what we already have, have less attachment to money, do not purposely disobey God, move in humility and fear of the Lord, and live our lives as close as we can to the Living Word of God (the Bible), then we will begin to experience a beautiful, wonderful life. To be experiencing anything less, we have to be actively resisting the blessings that are ready to be poured down from Heaven. The refusal of God's supernatural gifts is the most tragic mistake man can ever make. It is man who has to be remade first, then society will be remade by the restored, new man or woman. In most cases, mention of the word man refers to both genders. The constant refusal of man to receive a suprahistoric and supernatural power to break into his closed mind is the pride which prepares catastrophe. We all have been given freedom of choice. The choice is up to each and every individual on the face of this earth.

Escapists follow many different routes, but none of them are humble enough to admit that there is some evil in them. All of them are too proud to admit that they need outside help to cure their misery. By denying guilt, they show that they are cowards. By denying any perfection outside themselves, they become snobs. Escapists are pulled in two different directions at all times. They are not necessarily at ease with sin, but they are not so much in love with God that they disavow their faults. The desire to turn to God is there, but they do not have a sufficient amount of moral energy to be bad or to be good. They don't have enough religion to find true peace of soul, yet they have quite enough of it to intensify their sense of frustration after they have sinned. People who live in this moral dilemma between faith and lack of faith seldom have a clear notion of the purpose of life, yet we must have a goal before we can live. Unless a person is ready to ask for God's forgiveness of his sins, the examination of conscience may be only a vain form of introspection, which can make a soul worse if it ends in remorse instead of sorrow. In order to ever be able to love ourselves totally and to be able to look other people in the eye and connect with them in the spirit of love, we all need to be born again. It doesn't matter who a person is talking to, if a person has been born again, his spirit will bare witness of the love of Christ in the other person. They say the eyes are the windows of the soul. The love of Christ also shows in our voices. People who shine the love of Christ through them are easily trusted. If they abuse that trust from other people, then I can assure you that they will pay the consequences.

When I sold Medicare supplement insurance in the 1980s, I would go over all the benefits of my company and compare them with what the customer already had. As I began to close the sale, I always seemed to have a spirit of fear come over me. This was a fear of not making the sale. Actually, it was the rejection. My heart would begin to beat rapidly, and I would become anxious. If I allowed that fear to dominate and take control of all my thoughts, I did not make the sale. To all you salespeople out there, let me assure you that people are very smart. Most of the time they know whether or not we are being sincere. In reality, we are all salespeople who are trying to constantly sell our thoughts and our opinions to other people. If we are being sincere, we are usually relaxed, peaceful, friendly, and helpful. We can only show these traits to others if we have their interests before our own. If money is in the back of our minds all the time, then fear will invariably rear its ugly head just when we think we are about home free. Do any of you salespeople know what I am talking about? Sure you do. After my profound experience with the Lord in October of 1987, sales became easier than I ever could have imagined. I was learning to trust in the Lord by allowing His love to flow through me and by not being so self-confident. I was learning Christ-esteem, the total opposite of self-esteem. We must learn to dethrone self and put Christ back upon the throne. We must decrease. He must increase.

Chapter Five

The Spirit is Strong

I n today's pressure-cooker society, it seems that half the people want to sue or kill the other half. Where does one go to find peace in life? That question has only one answer, and His name is Jesus Christ. He is called "the Prince of Peace," among other names. He alone can give the peace that we all need to be able to rise above the adversities of life. It is very easy to be optimistic when your eyes are gazing continually up at Him. It is also very easy to become extremely pessimistic when you glance up at Him only occasionally. In *John 14: 27* Jesus said, *"My peace I give to you, not as the world giveth, give I unto you; let not your heart be troubled, neither let it be afraid."*

One of today's greatest fears is that of the unknown, the uncertainty, and the insecurity of tomorrow. God tells us not to be anxious about tomorrow and to live one day at a time. Worry accomplishes absolutely nothing. It will not add one single day to your life. In fact, enough worry will actually shorten your life, bringing upon you that which you worry about. Life is indeed a self-fulfilling prophecy. Worry is a sin. When you worry, you are, in essence, saying that your problems are much too big for the Lord to handle. *Psalms 37: 8* says, *"Don't fret and worry, it only leads to harm."* Of course you should have goals and plans, but you should not be so consumed with tomorrow that you lose today's joy and energy. If you cannot enjoy the journey toward your destination, then you certainly will not enjoy the destination when you get there. You are not guaranteed tomorrow; all you have is today. Worrying about tomorrow depletes your mental, physical, and spiritual energy today.

So many of today's health problems, especially heart attacks, can be related to worry and anxiety. Statistics show that eighty percent of the hospital beds are occupied by people with emotionally induced health problems. I am not saying that these problems are not real. However, many of these problems could have been avoided had some of these people learned how to slow down and enjoy life. Society teaches us to be independent and competitive, always striving for perfection. Society also teaches us that depending on God is a sign of weakness. This is such an incredible lie from Satan. Each of us has a deep desire to be able to tell every detail of our everyday lives to someone else. That is why each of us needs the Lord. He alone knows us inside and out and understands us completely. His love is unconditional. Satan tries to tell us that we are not worthy of approaching God, but *John 3: 16* says, *"For God so loved the world that He gave His only begotten Son, that whosoever believeth on Him should not perish, but have everlasting life."* Jesus was God manifested in the flesh, as outlined in the first chapter of *John*. When He arose from the dead and ascended back into Heaven, His Holy Spirit remained on earth. He is just as alive today as He was 2,000 years ago. His Spirit lives in the hearts and minds of every born-again Christian, guiding them daily into all truth and teaching them the true riches of eternal life.

God did not say that you have to straighten out every detail of your life before you can approach Him. It is true, as stated in *Romans 3: 23*, that each of us has sinned and fallen short of God's glory. Sin separates you from God and keeps you from being the person that God intends for you to be. When you invite Jesus into your heart, then you are endowed with His strength, and doubts begin to fade away. As I have already mentioned, the essence of Jesus cannot, by any means, be rationalized through the intellectual mind. He can be experienced only through the emotions of the heart and by inviting Him in and asking for forgiveness of your sins. However, you must be willing to forgive everyone who has ever hurt you in any way. You must confess Jesus as your Lord and Savior with your own words. *John 14: 6* says, *"Jesus is The Way, The Truth, and The Life, and no man cometh unto the Father except by Me."* Let that sink in for a minute. Are you wondering why God never seems to answer your prayers? Have you gone through His secretary? Unwillingness to forgive is the biggest obstacle to having your prayers answered. God is love. His Spirit is in everyone and becomes supercharged in those who have accepted Him as Savior. Therefore, if you are holding a grudge toward anyone for any reason, you are cutting yourself off from God. If you are wishing anything bad to happen to anyone, then you are wishing it for yourself. Judging others and thinking that they get what they deserve will likely cause you to experience something bad or unpleasant, and your prayers will not be readily answered. If you want your prayers answered more quickly, try praying for someone else. Try mentally forgiving other people. Try picturing them surrounded with joy, peace, good health, success, and a calm assurance.

Indeed, what you wish for others is inevitably what you will experience.

Each of us has the same basic drives, and they are:

1) Security

2) Recognition

3) Love

4) Adventure

5) The need to create

These drives are a part of human nature, and they are neither good nor evil. They just are. These drives will either push us into the arms of a loving Father, or if we do not look for answers to these drives in God, they will drive us into hell. Hell can, in one sense, be experienced right here on earth, but let me assure you that there is, indeed, a very real, eternal hell. When your basic human drives are not met in God, you feel inadequate or defeated. The whole world needs to be born again. People desperately need to get rid of the garbage of their past. In the person of Jesus Christ, you have been presented with the ultimate of God's excellence. Christ is a complete picture of excellence, of all that man can hope to become. It is in the light of this excellence that you can confront in yourself whatever limits you from rising to the fullest and the finest that you can be in Him. The human approach to a daily quest for excellence is often wearing. It is plagued with perfectionism, criticism, and competition. The divine way, however, is restful and is filled with grace, goodness, and mercy. The path of excellence is found through casting aside every evil pretension. The real possibility of glory will open only to those who renounce the notion that the flesh can attain it. This is accomplished through the confession of sin in prayer. The divine approach to excellence begins with bowing before the Lord.

God's supernatural power is always available to you. If you find yourself in a set of adverse circumstances and consciously choose to focus your thoughts on God, peace, and good will toward all those around you, the evil spirits will flee. However, given this same set of circumstances, if you begin to analyze everything and everyone and allow negative thoughts to slip in, then you may as well forget it. Choosing to center your mind on those things that are pure and lovely is one thing, but learning to stay there is a never-ending exercise. The Word of God is powerful. I remember a time when I was working at a furniture company, and business was slow. Several of us were standing around talking and waiting for customers to come in. The conversation became somewhat overheated very quickly. With an authoritative voice I said, "Peace, be still." The pow-wow broke up immediately. I noticed that everyone just sort of hung their heads and then turned and walked away. Satan recognizes the words of Jesus. Yes, as a born-again child of God, you have been given authority over Satan. He cannot stand for you to use the Word of God. Living in victory requires boldness and courage. I used to have heart palpitations quite frequently, and I learned to use those same words. The palpitations would stop immediately. There is indeed a connection between your thoughts, words, and actions and what you experience in this natural world inside and outside of your body. Modern medicine is beginning to acknowledge that prayer can help keep you in a sounder and healthier body.

A few years ago, during the first short-lived war over in Iraq, millions of people began to fervently seek some answers for themselves about these troubled times in which we live. With the quickening pace of life and world happenings, people were fleeing to bookstores, soaking up knowledge, and trying to figure out if the end of the world was at hand. No one knows when the end will come. There are many different beliefs surrounding this, but it is my understanding that the gospel of Christ must be preached to every corner of the world first, then Jesus will come again. I estimate that about thirty percent of the world has never heard the Gospel.

In 1991 there was a meeting of World Christian Evangelists who were already involved in carrying the Gospel around the world, and they came together to make strategic plans so that the Great Commission could be carried out more quickly and efficiently. How long do we have? No one knows. The end can come at anytime for anyone. Are you ready? Do you know Jesus as your personal Lord and Savior? Are you still trying to prolong the decision just as long as possible because you are afraid that you might have to give up some things that you really do enjoy? Perhaps you have already confessed Jesus as your Lord and Savior. If so, then this is the time to wean yourself from the milk and to begin eating the meat. The days of a person sitting on the fence are over. God said that He would rather us be cold than lukewarm. Otherwise He will spew us out of His mouth. He is shaking everything on this earth that can be shaken. It is not hard to see that this is true in every sense of the word. Look what happened September 11th, 2001. Terrorists were responsible for destroying the twin towers in New York City and thousands of people were killed. Take a look at what's happening in Israel. Hardly a day goes by without some terrible event happening in some part of our world. These are indeed perilous times in which we live. Being a Christian, though not always an easy road to follow, is far more rewarding than the alternative. Trials and tribulations come to Christians, and it is not easy to go through the fire, so to speak. As unpleasant as the fire is when you are going through it, those are the times when God is pulling you closer to Him and making you stronger and more aware of just how much you need Him in your life.

Now let us talk about applying the written Word of God to your daily life and learning how to stand firmly on the Word, trusting and believing God. Many wrong choices could be eliminated by spending time alone with God in prayer and praise and studying and applying His Word to your life. You need to daily seek God's purpose and will for your life. In order to be happy and to be in the perfect will of God, your soul, which is made up of your mind, your will, and your emotions, must come under subjection to the Holy Spirit. If you are walking in the Spirit, you are at peace inwardly and outwardly. Other people cannot easily cause you to feel anger, frustration, jealousy, envy, or resentment. Notice I said "easily." We are not perfect and we will slip out from under God's grace from time to time. In order for your emotions to be controlled by the Spirit, you must choose to feed your mind daily with God's Word and stay prayed up.

Simply reading is not enough. The Bible tells us that faith comes by hearing and hearing by the Word of God. Read that again. It says hearing, not reading. Your spirit picks up on things spoken (God's words) far more quickly and with much more depth of understanding when it is spoken, especially when you say it. When you hear a preacher begin to speak with more projection and volume as he or she dwells on a particular issue or point, he or she will become very excited. The words the preacher is speaking are registering in his or her own spirit, as well as to the audience, and many times more so, than with many of the people in the audience. However, those who have really been paying attention and following what the preacher has been saying also become very excited and find it difficult to sit still. Jesus is something to get excited about. I get concerned about those who just sit there Sunday after Sunday and never express any emotion at all. I feel really sad for them because they are not experiencing God fully, and it is no one's fault but their own. Choices are always there. Until people can make the decision to forget about the other people around them, they will never be able to enter fully into God's presence. One must lose consciousness of self before being able to focus fully on Christ and be able to worship Him the way He wants to be worshipped.

The word enthusiasm comes from the Greek word "enthos," which means in God. Enthusiasm is contagious.

If we all expressed as much enthusiasm for Jesus as we do for someone who makes a touchdown in a football game, what joy, peace, love, and harmony we all could enjoy! Holy Spirit revivals are happening all around the world as God pours out His Spirit on all flesh in the latter days as He said He would. Jesus is coming again soon, folks. We no longer will suffer heartaches, pain, or sorrow when Jesus comes again; eternal bliss through Jesus will be ours.

You must realize that God has done all that He is going to do for you; He sent His Son to die on the cross for you. He gave you the Bible as instructions for life. It contains every answer to every question, but it remains a mystery to understand unless Jesus lives in your heart. When the Spirit of the Living Lord merges with your spirit, the mysteries begin to unravel, and you begin to understand the Bible. When His promises have filled your heart and saturated your mind, the Holy Spirit will teach you how to apply those promises to your life. He will guide you into all Truth. God's Word is His will for your life. You have become a joint heir with Jesus and are worthy (only by the blood of Jesus) to receive all of God's promises. Your faith is activated fully as you set out to accomplish a certain task with expectations of a good outcome for all involved because you are standing on God's promises.

Yes, the spirit is strong, but the flesh is weak. The Spirit of our precious Lord and Savior is pulling us ever so gently toward our Father in Heaven. The fallen angel, Satan, who also has much power, though not nearly as much, is also pulling us, but in the opposite direction. He is trying to keep our minds on the wicked desires of the flesh. Many men and women experience feelings of worthlessness unless they have a wife or husband constantly demonstrating love or devotion. Don't get me wrong; there is nothing wrong with marriage. I was obviously just not good at it. However, I am certainly not the same person I used to be. Thank God He is in the people-changing business. *Matthew 19: 5* says that a man leaves home to take a wife. It is sad that most people follow their own will instead of God's will when choosing a mate; they very often make the wrong choice. Trying to change a mate can cause mental, emotional, or even physical suffering. As you already know, I am a perfect example of this scenario. In reality, the only one you can change is yourself. You must have a role model. You must have a desire that grows stronger everyday in order to become more and more like that role model. The perfect role model for the whole world is Jesus Christ. God knows that no one is perfect. However, His desire is that each of us strives for perfection, forgiving others and self daily. You must realize that you need help to overcome any bad habit, whether it be smoking, alcohol, drug abuse, overeating, overspending, or any other weakness you might have. I had tried many times on my own to quit smoking. It did not work until I got down on my knees and cried out to God to remove the desire for cigarettes. God delivered me from cigarettes. That was in 1992. I had been addicted for twenty-eight years, and I can say truthfully that, since then, I have never wanted another one.

You need a strength outside yourself to help you overcome life's problems. That strength comes from a personal relationship with Jesus Christ. This is where salvation from God comes in. Even after salvation, one still feels the inner struggle between the spirit and the desires of the flesh, and many occasionally, at least at first, slip back into their old ways. After awhile you realize that the mental, physical, spiritual, emotional, and financial aspects of life are far more rewarding when you daily strive to live in the path of righteousness. Allowing Satan to pull us back down into old patterns of living is self-defeating and humiliating. The result is never what we hoped it would be. Why? Because we were listening to the wrong voice, and we certainly were not in the will of God. Happiness and freedom come only when the will of self dies, allowing the will of God to live.

How does this happen? You first must accept Jesus into your heart and confess Him as your Lord and Savior. You must associate with other believers and spend time alone with the Lord in Bible study, prayer, and praise. In order to reap the highest rewards, I urge you to make time for these activities daily without fail. *Isaiah 26: 3* tells us that the enemy, Satan, comes to steal, to kill, and to destroy. Daily worship will help to guard against Satan's attacks. The battleground starts in the mind, and God says that He will keep those in perfect peace whose mind is stayed on Him.

Satan's numerous, ever-present temptations are trying to destroy us. His ways are very subtle, and unless you seek guidance and wisdom daily through prayer, you can get caught up in a whirlwind of unpleasant circumstances. You have choices as to what thoughts you will allow your mind to entertain. Thoughts are powerful; thoughts are energy. Satan may plant immoral thoughts in your mind, but you can simply command him to get out of your life in the name of Jesus. Resist the devil, and he will flee from you. I did not say that; God did. Thoughts can be used to create beautiful, happy events or to create ugliness. The choice is up to each individual. The flesh will follow the path created by the thought patterns of each individual. You do not have to entertain bad thoughts. When bad thoughts enter your mind, you can train yourself to say, "Lord, I give You this thought," and you can immediately direct your thoughts to something beautiful. You do have a choice. Because of the sin nature of man handed down from Adam and Eve, you cannot keep bad thoughts from coming occasionally, but you can turn those thoughts over to God and refocus on something good. It is your advantage to do so because you are continually creating events and circumstances for your future with your thoughts, words, and actions.

Resisting change is normal. Getting older seems to bring more resistance to change. Change means uncertainty. Fear of the unknown is very real. It is much easier to cling to old, familiar ways than it is to accept new ways. Giving up old ways and habits can seem quite threatening. You might wonder if you will still be happy or if others will still like you if you change. Nevertheless, God reminds us that every person is created in His image and for His pleasure. God allows you to make choices, but if you make the wrong choices, you can choose to learn from your mistakes, or you can keep making the same mistakes over and over. If you learn what you are supposed to learn, you move on to a higher consciousness, temporarily thinking you have the world by the tail. You think you know all you need to know. You drift along for awhile with some successes, and you sort of tend to forget about God, the One Who put you back on the right track. You try to mold Him into being what you want Him to be. Life just does not work that way. You are not here on this earth to see how much wealth you can accumulate or how many possessions you can buy before you die. The last clothes you wear will have no pockets; you will take nothing with you. Although God does want you to prosper in every way, you are here for one reason. That reason is to learn to become more like Jesus; patient, loving, kind, forgiving, bearing one another's burdens, exhorting and encouraging one another, and living in peace, love, and harmony until Jesus returns. Then everyone will know that He is King of Kings and Lord of Lords. Jesus is the example by which you can determine whether or not you are on the path to excellence. Don't get caught up comparing yourself to other people. We must examine ourselves only in the light of Jesus Christ. We are all unique individuals because God created us that way. When He comes again, there will be total peace, love, and harmony on earth for one thousand years.

The firm foundation on which Christianity is built is forgiveness. *John 3: 16* says, *"For God so loved the world that He gave His only begotten Son that whosoever believeth in Him should not perish, but have everlasting life."* We either accept that as the truth, or we are calling God a liar. I know without a doubt that this is the Truth. However, before October, 1987, I had my doubts. When a person desires wisdom just as much as the air he breathes, then and only then will wisdom he receive.

In the Lord's prayer, as outlined in *Matthew 6: 14*, God said, *"For if ye forgive men their trespasses, your Heavenly Father will also forgive you."* The next verse tells us, *"If ye forgive not men their trespasses, neither will your Father forgive your trespasses."* I have learned, for my sake and for Christ's sake, that I must forgive everyone who has ever hurt me. Each of us must realize that we cannot do this in our own strength; we are capable of this only when Jesus Christ is living in us. God will forgive us when we forgive others. Holding grudges is a sin, and sin keeps us separated from God. Unrepented sin keeps us from fully experiencing God and His blessings.

Matthew 18: 21-22 tells of Peter's question to Jesus about forgiveness: *"Then came Peter to Him, and said, Lord, how oft shall my brother sin against me, and I forgive him? till seven times? Jesus saith unto him, I say not unto thee, Until seven times: but, Until seventy times seven."* In other words, God wants us to forgive others every time we are hurt. I do not think that He wants us to count each hurt up to 490 times.

We would have to keep books on that. That is not what He meant, praise God!

According to *Ephesians 4: 32,* we should *"Be ye kind one to another, tenderhearted, forgiving one another, even as God for Christ's sake hath forgiven you."* In 1992, when I sold furniture for a local retailer in Dothan, Alabama, there were occasional disagreements among the salespeople. One lady had sold furniture for over twenty years and had built a very good customer base. Most of the customers asked for her by name when they came back. However, they were sometimes assisted by other salespeople. They would not buy right away, and when they did return, they would ask for the person who normally assisted them, and she would get the sale. Situations like this were rare and usually unavoidable; nevertheless, the feelings of the other salespeople were hurt, and your faith is put to the test in situations like these. Working strictly commission, as most salespeople do, caused a lot of hard feelings when those situations arose. I learned a lot about trusting God at this place. Harboring resentment blocked God's blessings from me. However, praying that God would bless the other salesperson and the customer brought me countless blessings in the form of sales that were just as good and sometimes better. God is awesome, and He knows our needs. His desire is that we trust Him and love others all the time. *Romans 12: 21* advises us to *"Be not overcome of evil, but overcome evil with good."* God blesses us tremendously when we exhibit faith in Him.

Romans 10: 17 says that *"Faith cometh by hearing and hearing by the Word of God."* It is not enough to hear the Word occasionally; a happy, peaceful, and prosperous life on earth requires hiding the Word in your heart, keeping it continually before your eyes, and meditating upon it. You must allow the Holy Spirit to speak to you through the Word. After you have accepted Jesus, you will always know when you need to forgive someone. When you begin to hold a grudge, guilt will rear its ugly head. This is a sign of conviction. It is best to choose to forgive and to let it go. Understand that people will always disappoint you, but God is always right there for you. His open arms are always there to hold you and to comfort you. Do not let bitterness set in; it will destroy you.

Perfection does not exist in human beings. The cleansing of forgiveness is a continual process; you must seek it daily. This does not mean that you have free reign to sin against God. It means that each of us, imperfect as we are, will find it easy to fall short of the Glory of God. You will be much happier if you are quick to repent. You might be surprised at what happens if you pray for the other person. God can take a situation and turn it around completely for the benefit of all concerned. He has all the right answers, and He does, indeed, work in mysterious ways. God answers the prayer of the pure in heart. He favors and blesses those that keep Him foremost in their thoughts and hearts.

Holding grudges and resentment toward others definitely will block the flow of blessings into your life. You must wish joy, peace, success, love, and harmony for those that you think of or talk to daily. Other than blasphemy of the Holy Spirit, I believe that unforgiveness is the worst sin. Actually, sin is sin. Blasphemy is the only unpardonable sin. *Romans 6: 23* plainly states, *"For the wages of sin is death; but the gift of God is eternal life through Jesus Christ our Lord."* This eternal life comes from knowing Jesus Christ as personal Lord and Savior. Learning to forgive is not an option. It is imperative if you want the blessings of God to flow in your life. You cannot forgive others on your own. It requires humbling yourself before the Lord and asking Him to help you. Jesus died on the cross for all the whole world and yet just before He died He asked God to forgive the ones who were killing Him. Unforgiveness is like drinking a glass of poison and expecting the other person to die. Rest in the assurance of *Philippians 4: 13: "I can do all things through Christ Who strengtheneth me."*

Proverbs 15: 15 says that *"He that hath a merry heart hath a continual feast."* It does not say that you can have a feast and then be happy. You must be happy first. It is a choice. However, if you are holding grudges against other people, chances are likely that you go through life most of the time looking like a sourpuss. I do not think that a continual feast is very likely under these circumstances. God sees our hearts. You cannot hide any thoughts or feelings from Him. He owns everything; we will play by His rules, or else we will lose the game. Humble yourself before Him, or He will humble you. If you are quick to judge yourself, then God will not have to. There is a universal law at work, whether you acknowledge it or not. If you wake up in a joyful, peaceful state of mind (or at least try to accomplish this through prayer before you leave home), you will attract joyful, peaceful, trusting people into your life. We are like a magnet. What we send out comes right back to us. If we sow discord, we will reap discord. This happens with absolutely no exceptions. Sowing discord among brethren is one of the things that God hates according to His Word.

Since it takes more effort to be grouchy, bitter, and fearful, it only makes sense to do what is necessary to develop a joyful state of mind before you talk to the first person everyday. *Nehemiah 2: 10* says, *"The joy of the Lord is our strength."* If we want life to be joyful, peaceful, and happy, it must begin with us. Don't expect others to make you happy. Their humanness will cause them to always fall short of the goals and your expectations. If your inner self is right, then the outer world will be right. Keeping your mind focused on the shortcomings of others and why they cannot, or will not, do as you think they should will magnify and multiply what you see as a problem. On the flip side, if you can tune your thoughts to the beautiful, abundant, wonderful world in which you live and the opportunities available to you each day, you will be much happier. I have found that I wake up in a more positive mood if I do not go to bed with bad feelings toward anyone. If anyone hurts you lift that person up in prayer with forgiveness in your heart so that you can have a good night's sleep. Worrying about what someone has or has not done, or what someone may or may not do, will not add one minute to your life. On the contrary, it will subtract from it.

You occasionally will run into those who have less than a sunny outlook on life, and they will probably rub your spirit the wrong way. You can learn to look behind their anger, frustration, irritability, or whatever they may be revealing to you and make a major difference in their lives. In fact, that is why God sometimes puts those people in our paths.

It is a training ground for us. Everyone needs other people; everyone needs encouragement. Think back to when someone reached out to you and encouraged you. Do the same thing for someone else. Do not react to how that person is acting, but respond with love. You can do it if you walk closely with Jesus everyday. Remember that God's purpose always stands through the storm. As a born-again Christian, you have been given the power to claim victory over the adverse situations in the name of Jesus. Jesus' name has far more power than most people ever could imagine. If you think all of this sounds too good to be true and that no one understands what you are going through, rest assured that God does understand even if those around you do not. The circumstances of your life happen for a reason, and God understands all of this. You will learn from these circum-stances only if you choose to be enlightened. You only have to ask God, and He will reveal the answers to you in His good time. *James 4: 2* says, *"We have not because we ask not."* I am not saying that God puts bad things in our lives. He wants only good things for us. Your own choices bring about sticky situations from time to time. If we obey the promptings of the Holy Spirit more often, then we experi-ence sticky situations less and less.

125

If we are choosing to walk in the spirit of love, daily forgiving one another, then we are opening ourselves up to receive blessings from God. However, if we are holding grudges, resentment, and hostility toward others, then we are blocking the blessings that God wants to shower upon us. We all need to learn how to allow God's love to flow into and through us. This will happen only if we spend time with Him in private and corporate worship. Because of all the negativity in this world and the problems that bombard us everyday from every direction, we need to constantly be refilled with God's love and energy. This can happen only by spending time alone with Him. He said, *"Be still and know that I am God."*

Yes, the spirit is strong, but the flesh is weak. The flesh is actually a negative way of thinking. This is indeed totally opposite of what God wants. He has given us so many wonderful, beautiful promises. In order to receive them we must BELIEVE them and the first pre-requisite is to stay in obedience to Him. To fear the Lord is the beginning of wisdom.

Chapter Six

The Power of Your Words

Most people do not realize just how powerful their words are. You are a co-creator with God, for He has made you in His image. Every word coming out of your mouth is planting seeds of faith, which is what God honors, or feeding negative energy to fear-filled situations involving you or someone you know. Of all the chapters in this book, this one alone can dramatically change the course of your life for the better if you will grab hold in your spirit the message that is presented here.

Before the human race ever existed, there was only darkness. God spoke the world into existence from the very beginning. He said, according to *Genesis 1: 3, "Let there be light; and there was light." John 1: 1-3 tells us, "In the beginning was the Word, and the Word was with God, and the Word was God. The same was in the beginning with God. All things were made by Him; and without Him was not any thing made that was made."* God spoke to Mary and told her that she would conceive a son in her womb, and He spoke Jesus into being. However, Mary had to *first believe the Word of God.* She had to believe that she had conceived the Word, which is Jesus, into her womb. The Bible makes it very clear that the Word is God, and the Word was with God. Jesus was with God; Jesus is the Word. It is the most powerful Word in the universe. It is a name that is exalted far above any name we could ever speak and of course is the name most highly recognized throughout all the world. Just speaking Jesus' name releases a tremendous amount of supernatural power. It is as though His spirit lives in the ethers of this universe, and indeed it does. When we speak His name, it seems to bring Him onto the scene instantly in that given set of circumstances, restoring peace, grace, and love. Just thinking about Him brings the same results. He said, *I will keep thee in perfect peace whose mind is stayed on Me."*

The Bible says that the Word became flesh and dwelt among us. This flesh refers to Jesus, so it's time we all learn how powerful the words are that we speak, and if we can get ourselves into a position where we are lining up with the Word of God, then we can bring about many wonderful

things for ourselves and for mankind. We are deceiving ourselves if we think we are just out here, living randomly and
waiting for things to happen without control. This is not true.
There are laws of cause and effect at work. Every choice we
make will have a consequence. If we are staying close to
Jesus and seeking guidance from the Holy Spirit, then we
are building precept upon precept, line upon line, and we
are living in the will of God. Then again, if we are never
spending time alone with the Lord and are doing all these
things everyday with no forethought as to what God wants
us to do that day, then we are living in our own wills and
cannot experience the true blessings that God has in store
for us.

The Bible admonishes us about our words in *Psalms 19:
14: "Let the words of my mouth, and the meditation of my
heart, be acceptable in thy sight, O Lord, my strength, and
my redeemer." Psalms 141: 3* tells us that we should ask
for God's help in controlling our words: *"Set a watch, O
Lord, before my mouth; keep the door of my lips."* In *John
6: 63* Jesus said, *"the words that I speak unto you, they are
spirit, and they are life." Proverbs 18: 21* warns, *"Death
and life are in the power of the tongue..."* Think about these
last two verses. When you get hold of what God is saying,
you will have discovered the main keys to the Kingdom of

God, and you will learn how to tap into the storehouse of infinite wisdom and bring God on the scene in your behalf, no matter what circumstances you may be going through. Now, if God's words are life and there is life in the power of the tongue, doesn't it make sense that He has given us the key to create just about anything we want to, provided it is for the good of all and not for evil? Although God gives us these powers, they are a function of faith in God.

One cannot function at all without certain amounts of faith. It takes faith to walk across the room to turn on a light switch and expect the light to come on. A person simply cannot have faith and fear on the inside at the same time. *Hebrews 11: 6* tells us that it is impossible to please God without faith. Faith comes by hearing and hearing by the Word of God. It doesn't come by having heard it once or by hearing it occasionally.

It comes by hearing it over and over and over. It would be great to hear the Word once and have all the faith we need to do everything we want to do. However, God didn't design things that way. He's a very jealous God. He will have our attention one way or another, and rightfully so. He is worthy, His faithfulness is great, and His mercy endures forever. We can attain a certain amount of faith by listening to preachers or other inspirational speakers. However, we tend to believe our own words far more quickly than what anyone else says. With that in mind, listen closely here. Let this sink into your spirit. When you speak what God said (His covenant promises) with authority in your own voice, nothing makes Satan any madder, and he has no choice but to flee from you. When you speak what God said into a given situation, it is as though every angel on earth goes to work for you to bring to pass what you are saying. Things may happen quickly, or it may take longer, depending on where a person is on his level of faith. It is a process, a new way of life that must be developed over time. *Matthew 9: 29* promises, *"According to your faith be it unto you."* It will not be done unto you according to anyone else's faith, although their prayers most assuredly can bring you much closer to God. If you are in fear of something bad happening, then you are using perverted faith. You are believing in a negative outcome, and you are not trusting God and obviously not confessing His Word to bring Him to your aid. God has already done everything He is going to do for mankind. He loved us so much that He gave His only Son for our sins, sicknesses, diseases, and poverty. What more could He do? He gave us a book of instructions to use for every situation in our lives. It is up to each and every individual to apply the Living Word of God to his/her own life. We have all learned different levels of faith, and what we must learn to do is to stretch the faith that we presently have in order to receive anything more than we presently have. We cannot make other people operate on our level of faith. There are facts here in this natural world, but the power of the spiritual world can overcome the natural. God's Word is the truth. His truth far supersedes any so-called facts on the physical plane. Learn to stretch your faith, and learn how to apply God's Word to your life. Since God made us in His image, we have been made partakers of His divine nature. When we speak what He says, those words which are His Spirit go deep down into our spirits, resting in our hearts, and faith builds every time we do this. Jesus said in *Matthew 17: 20, "If ye have faith as a grain of mustard seed, ye shall say unto this mountain, Remove hence to yonder place; and it shall remove; and nothing shall be impossible unto you."* Now let that verse grab hold of you. He says that you can speak directly to the problem and command it to be removed, in the name of Jesus, of course, and it would have to go. However, for this to work for you, you must not doubt that it will work. You must believe it. We cannot be double-minded and expect to receive anything from God.

Have you noticed how I keep mentioning the word believe? Why do you suppose Christians are called believers? They have reached a point in their walk with the Lord where they have chosen to believe God's Word, regardless of circumstances because, primarily through many trials and errors, they have come to experience the power of God's Word in their lives. You can, too, but you must first and foremost choose to believe on the Lord Jesus Christ. If you believe in Him, on Him, and in the power of His blood, then as God said in *Matthew 19: 26, "with God all things are possible."* There have been numerous occasions when I have applied God's Word to my own circumstances. For instance, I have faced matters or situations that were foreign to me or perhaps something I had done many times before, but fear still tried to creep in. I would repeat over and over until I felt peace, "His grace is sufficient for me." Fear seems to try to take over sometimes, but Jesus said in *2 Corinthians 12: 9* that His grace is sufficient for us to be able to go through anything. Another wonderful verse that I apply quite often to my life is *1 John 4: 4, "Greater is He that is in me, than he that is in the world."* Satan cannot destroy your peace when you are under the grace of God. We can walk under God's grace more often by staying close to Jesus. I have found that these perilous times in which we live require staying very close to Him. As I quoted previously in this chapter, *Proverbs 18: 21* speaks of the death and life that is held in the power of the tongue. Negative self-talk will produce death of your dreams and worthwhile goals as well as of your body. Positive self-talk will produce positive things and circumstances for you. Develop an attitude of gratitude. Attitude is everything. Speak words of love. Speak God's Word; speak His promises and personalize them. We must teach our minds to expect good things by speaking only good things concerning ourselves and others. Faith is a process. It must be built. It won't happen overnight. You can start small. For example, the next time you pull into a shopping center parking lot, try thanking God for a parking space up close. You must believe you will receive before you actually receive anything from God. The believing must come first. God honors faith; He wants us to trust Him. He wants us to trust in His Living Word. It is just that simple. His Word is powerful. It can break every yoke of bondage, but we must apply His Word. Work the Word, and it will work for you. Be careful not to let this become just a ritualistic practice. Remember, God is jealous.

If you are truly ready to put yourself in a position to claim your rightful, divine inheritance, then all you have to do is to confess your sins to the Lord and invite Him into your heart to be Lord of your life. Ask Him to reveal Himself to you. Forgive others who have hurt you. You may think you can never forgive those who have hurt you. Ask the Lord to help you forgive them. You will begin to see that as you truly learn to lean on the Lord and on His Word that you can trust Him. *Psalms 37: 4* says, *"Delight thyself also in the Lord; and He shall give thee the desires of thine heart."* That sounds like another blank check from heaven to me. Yes, Jesus is the way, the truth, and the life. No beautiful car, no fancy house, or no powerful position with any company can ever satisfy or fill the void in the human heart. Only Jesus can do that. We are created this way. The human spirit longs to be close to Him. We will always have the feeling of never quite being there. We are filled with His love and His peace, but it is an ongoing experience. We know we must continue on the path of righteousness. We must be in a constant state of transformation and in a constant state of expectation (faith). Faith without works is dead. Working your faith means staying in the Living Word of God, applying the principles of prosperity, and claiming the promises of God. Faith requires action. Without action towards a positive expectation, there is no faith. Faith, however, should not be confused with hope.

There is a difference between hope and faith. Hope is for the future. Faith is applied in the present. *Hebrews 11: 1* tells us that *"faith is the substance of things hoped for, the evidence of things not seen."* Applied faith is standing on the Word of God, not the facts as we actually see them in the natural world. We are to work our faith by quoting God's words as they are in the Bible and claiming specific things we desire, as long as those things are for good and not evil. Apply 100% of your belief (faith) behind what you are saying and stand firmly, trusting God. A key point to remember is that you must never resent other people for the money they earn, and you must never waver in your faith. When Satan tries to tell you there is no way, tell him to get out of your life in the name of Jesus. If you are believing one minute and doubting the next, then you will cancel out the applied faith. Stand firmly on God's Word. It will happen for you. Claim God's promise in *Matthew 9: 29: "According to your faith be it unto you."* Also remember *Proverbs 23: 7: "For as he thinketh in his heart, so is he..."* The book of *Proverbs* is rich in helping one learn how to achieve understanding:

Proverbs 2: 10-12: "When wisdom entereth into thine heart, and knowledge is pleasant unto thy soul; discretion shall preserve thee, understanding shall keep thee: to deliver thee from the way of the evil man, from the man that speaketh froward things."

Proverbs 3: 5-6: "Trust in the Lord with all thine heart; and lean not unto thine own understanding. In all

*thy ways acknowledge Him, and He shall direct thy
paths."*

*Proverbs 3: 13: "Happy is the man that findeth wisdom, and
the man that getteth understanding."*

The first thing I urge each and every one of you to do
right now is to make a firm decision to eliminate these words
from your vocabulary: 1) I'm broke. 2) I can't. 3) I'm sick.
In fact, once you begin to understand the power of your
words upon your circumstances, you will indeed refrain
from stating anything that is negative concerning yourself.
Don't even jokingly say anything negative about yourself
or other people. I'll explain why later, but for now, I would
like for you to understand that you are much more than the
little physical package you walk around in. You are a multi-
dimensional being made up of spirit, mind, and body, and
you have been given a tool one million times more powerful than any man-made computer, your brain, which has
different levels of consciousness. The saddest thing in the
world to me is a person who does not take the time to understand anything at all about how the brain works. Your subconscious mind cannot distinguish between a joke or what
you really desire. *Romans 12: 2* says, *"And be not conformed to this world; but be ye transformed by the renewing*

of your mind..." People who are conformed to this world are constantly stating things (the facts) as they actually are in the natural world. Living as flesh and blood human beings, it is very easy for people to get caught up in the habit of stating exactly how they may presently feel, sometimes describing every detail of their pain. We tend to want to justify to ourselves our lack of productivity or to others why we find ourselves in the situation that we are in or the lack of joy in our lives. The devil loves this. God wants to hear us say the truth. His Word says to call things as though they are, in other words to call them as though you want them to be. Declare it, and stand firmly on His promises, regardless of how you feel. God's truth will always override the facts, but we must not give up, no matter what or no matter how long it may take to see or feel a substantial difference in our bodies or in our lives. There is much wisdom in the old adage that if we can't say anything good about anyone, then don't say anything. This includes ourselves. Quit sabotaging yourself with all the negatives going into your subconscious mind. If you keep saying you are broke, I can assure you that you will eventually end up broke. You will always be in a state of lack. Your subconscious mind will cause you to take actions that will cause you to end up broke. I believe it was Napoleon Hill who said, "Whatever the mind of man can conceive and believe, it can achieve." The founder of Combine Insurance Company, W. Clement Stone, understood the powerful principles of success as outlined in the Bible and applied them. Of course, I think we all know how successful he was. He was a born-again Christian who started his company with $100.00. If you have never read his book, *The Successful System That Never Fails,* you owe it to yourself to do so.

Yes, the human brain, designed by the Master of all creation, was designed in such a way that the subconscious mind accepts whatever you say as a direct command and will bring to pass that which you say, sooner or later, whether you were joking or not. I know you're thinking that you're not supposed to lie. My dear friend, standing on the Word of God is "the truth," not a lie. Don't listen to Satan trying to twist your mind so that he can keep you caught up in a state of financial lack, poverty, and sickness. I was raised in the traditional Methodist Church, but once I received the baptism of the Holy Spirit, the mysteries of the Kingdom of God began to unveil themselves to me as the Bible stated they would in *Mark 4: 11-32.* As I said before, I don't claim to have all the answers. What I am saying is that the Holy Spirit is the greatest teacher of all. He is available to you right now, but He will enter your spirit only with your permission. The Holy Spirit led me into the Pentacostal movement. The majority of these people have been fully emerged in the spirit, as opposed to the majority of the people in traditional churches. Once a person has been baptized in the Holy Spirit, it is very hard for that person to be ministered to if attending a very ritualistic, humdrum church, because such churches do not openly worship God the way that He desires to be worshipped, with hands being raised as a symbol of surrender to God or as outlined in *Psalms 150.* I don't mean to imply that there aren't Spirit-filled people in these other churches; there certainly are. Most every church today has at least a little group of Spirit-filled people because God is pouring out His Spirit on earth as He said He would in these last days. However, on any given day no one has any more of the Holy Spirit than what they have yielded themselves to be filled with for that day. Depending on how long they have closely walked with the Lord will determine their level of maturity.

Every church teaches positive affirmations. Positive affirmations repeated daily and entering your subconscious mind will eventually produce the things you are programming into it. Most people, however, are caught up in rationalizing everything to death. They stay in limbo, never really achieving anything worthwhile in life. We must understand right now, my friend, that Satan wants to destroy you and me. He wants to see us in poverty, sickness, disease, and death, never having accomplished anything for mankind. Yes, it is a natural human response to weigh the facts (reality), but if you have a worthwhile idea, a workable plan, and a burning desire to make it come true, please know that God does not give people an impossible idea. Sure, there will be setbacks and problems along the way, but you must keep your faith; never give in to the fears and doubts coming from none other than Satan. If we do, we will fail. Keep in mind *Matthew 19: 26* that tells us that all things are possible with God. *Deuteronomy 8: 18* says it is God Who has given us the power to get wealth. We must be thankful for everything, even the problems. God allows problems in our lives to help us to grow and to mature and to learn to lean more on Him. We must daily ask for forgiveness and forgive others. Carrying around a suitcase full of bitterness, anger, hate, hostility, or negative feelings toward anyone will block the blessings God wants to give to us. Remember, He holds the purse strings. We need to begin to look at all the beauty in the world. *Proverbs 22: 4* says, *"By humility and the fear of the Lord are riches, and honour, and life."* Jesus said, *"I have come that ye might have life, and ye might have it more abundantly."* Jesus is the symbol that we must all look up to in order to gauge where we are in our transformation. All of us were created with the inborn desire to grow closer and closer to God. As long as we deny Him, He will deny us. Jesus said that He and the Father are one; no one comes to the Father except by Him. Remember Buddha, Mohammad, nor Allah died for us. Jesus did. Freedom is found only through a very close relationship with Jesus Christ. If you are truly ready to accept all your divine inheritance from God, then your mind and your heart must be pure. Yes, all of us have come short of the glory of God. Sometimes it seems as though the message being given is that there is virtue in poverty, but this is not true. Money is not the root of all evil, the love of money is. Money is the substance which God places in our hands according to His riches in glory, and money is what can help millions and millions of people in this world to find shelter and clothing. Hoarding money is what causes a recession. Money must be continually flowing in and out of a person's life. It must continue to circulate. The Bible says in *Job 22: 28, "Thou shalt also decree a thing, and it shall be established unto thee; and the light shall shine upon thy ways."* This is another way of saying what you say is what you get. Please understand that your praying and your saying must be the same. Control your thoughts; it is possible. It may be difficult at first, but practice makes perfect. All things be right if the mind be so. I know you have heard the old saying that two heads are better than one. This saying actually came from the Bible. *Matthew 18: 19* tells us, *"That if two of you shall agree on earth as touching any thing that they shall ask, it shall be done for them of My Father which is in heaven."* A lot of married couples know how to apply this principle. However, the problem is that one of them begins to take credit for the good outcome, not giving God the glory. As we learn to do the things that are right in our own heart (being led by the Holy Spirit), then we are building character, and we are walking in love under the anointing of grace from Almighty God. Fear will become almost foreign to you. You will begin to recognize all the subtle tricks that Satan uses to keep people in bondage to fear, doubt, depression, anger, etc.

Yes, God gave you freedom of choice. Over 80% of our circumstances are generated by our own self-talk and the images we hold in our mind. If we are showing that same old horror movie we starred in over two years ago over and over in our mind, then no wonder we are at our wits' end just struggling every day. We need to stop blocking God's blessings. We need to take control of our thoughts and our words. It's up to you and me. You *are* special. God's Word says you are. It is the truth, no matter what anyone says. His Word is His will for you. You must work His Word to be able to receive your inheritance. Stop for a minute and think about everything in this world. Every building, every structure of any kind has to have first begun as a thought in someone's mind, or else it would not be here today. Contemplate these ideas:

Sow a thought; reap an action.

Sow an action; reap a habit.

Sow a habit; reap a character.

Sow a character; reap a destiny.

The choice is up to us. There is a price to pay either way you go. Do you want to pay the price for eternal, true riches and also be blessed to the fullest here on Earth, or do you want to listen to Satan filling your mind with fears and doubts? We need to guard what goes into our minds. If garbage goes in, garbage will come out of our mouths. We must be good finders. Look for the good in everything and everybody. This does not mean that you have to be anyone's doormat. Guard your time wisely. Don't let other people waste it with malicious gossip or trivial conversation. Of course you don't have to be rude to people. If you can give a few words of encouragement, do a good deed for someone, show love towards someone, or lead someone to Christ, then by all means do so. The Holy Spirit will guide you if you ask

Him. That's what life is all about. The Holy Spirit will guide you in all matters, including confession.

There are two types of confession. The confession of our sins to God is for the cleansing of sins and guilt. The other type of confession is the confession of God's Word, speaking His Holy Word, which is powerful. There truly is death and life in the power of the tongue, and the second part of *Proverbs 18: 21* says, *"and they that love it shall eat the fruit thereof."* If we are quoting words of the devil, which are full of fear, hate, or hostility, then we are releasing the ability of the devil to accomplish that about which we are talking. We must understand that every word we speak is producing either fear or faith, it's just that simple.

The Word of God, conceived in the human spirit, formed with the tongue, and spoken out of the mouth, releases the ability of God to work on our behalf. We need to learn how to get our spoken words in line with what God says. Then it becomes a spiritual force for good. Every seed produces after its kind. Whatever kinds of seeds we plant will be exactly what we should expect to harvest. If you are speaking fear-filled words about yourself or about someone else, then you are feeding back into your spirit bad seeds which will grow to produce less than desirable circumstances either that day or in the future. If you are speaking words of love, faith, encouragement, inspiration, etc., then you are planting wonderful seeds. You are raising the expectations of yourself and others. You are building bridges instead of walls. We must be careful when we are joking because our tongues can deceive our hearts into believing that the words spoken are exactly what we want, and our spirits will say, "Let's find a way to bring that to pass." I'm telling you that we need to learn how powerful our words are. We are creating our own little world. Are you creating yours the way you want it to be in the future? Seeds are being planted for good or for bad all the time. Every word is a potential seed. When you operate a spiritual law, you have an incorruptible seed. When you speak God's Word, that is an incorruptible seed that will always work. That doesn't mean that you will always have the harvest you intended. You can do things to stop the harvest, but you can't stop the seed from working. It will do its part.

I challenge you right now to personalize this Bible verse. Start going through your day periodically saying, "My God supplies all my needs according to His riches in glory by Christ Jesus." As you begin to give God credit for all the good and wonderful blessings, just watch how much more abundantly you will be blessed in all areas of your life. You will be amazed at all the little miracles that begin to happen.

God wants to pour out to you blessing so abundant that there won't be room enough to receive them. A good man out of the good treasure of his heart brings forth good things. Speaking God's Word out of our own mouths does several things. We are planting seeds. Those seeds will build our faith more and more as time goes on, and faith is what will bring God on the scene in our behalf, provided we are praying for the good of all parties involved. Learn to take dominion over your words. Uncontrolled power is just allowing any words to roll off your tongue with no forethought as to the damage this can cause not only to others, but to yourself as well. Negative words towards and about others can and will boomerang right back to us. Uncontrolled power will destroy. You have power available to you through God's Living Word. We all have power through our words, and unless that power is controlled, we can cause ourselves a tremendous amount of problems. The Bible tells us in *John 6: 63, "It is the Spirit that quickeneth; the flesh profiteth nothing: the words that I speak unto you, they are spirit, and they are life."* It is extremely important for us to agree with God and to say what God says. God desires to do many things for us, but we need to come into agreement with Him, or these wonderful things will never come to pass. When it comes to the promises of God and entering into the provisions that God has made, then your words, spoken in belief, can change it for the better, or you can change it for the worse.

Now let's go back to how Jesus was conceived. The first chapter of *Luke* describes how the angels came to Mary and said, " *'Hail, thou art highly favored. The Lord is with thee. Blessed art thou among women', and the angel said unto her, 'Fear not, Mary, for thou has found favor with God, and behold, thou shalt conceive in thy womb and bring forth a son and shall call His name Jesus. He shall be great and He shall be called the Son of the Highest and the Lord God shall give unto Him the throne of His father, David, and He shall reign over the house of Jacob forever, and in His Kingdom there shall be no end.'"* Notice that Mary did not convey unbelief, but she asked a question: *"How shall this be, seeing I know not a man?"* The angel answered and said unto her, *"The Holy Ghost shall come upon thee, and the power of the Highest shall overshadow thee. Therefore, also, that Holy thing which shall be born of thee shall be called the Son of God."* Mary answered, *"Behold the handmaid of the Lord, be it done unto me according to Thy Word,"* and then the angel departed from her. Mary conceived the Word of God. She actually conceived God's Word sent by an angel, and she simply agreed with God after the angel explained that this would be an act of the Holy Spirit. The Holy Spirit is the author of the Word of God.

Faith is the ability to conceive what God has declared. Mary heard the Word. She conceived the Word. She received the Word into her spirit, and she spoke it!! She had no evidence that this would come to pass. All she had was the Word of God. Faith gave her the ability to conceive God's Word in her spirit. There is spirit life in God's Word. There is a faith force, a spiritual power that's capable of bringing to pass what God has promised, but it has to be received. It has to be conceived in the human spirit of the heart. Yes, what we say is indeed what we get, so get the right words coming out of your mouth, God's words. Come into agreement with Him. He said, *"Beloved, I wish above all things that thou mayest prosper and be in good health."* Remember: What the mind seeks the mouth speaks. What the mouth speaks the brain records. What the brain records the body manifests.

Chapter Seven

Prayer and Spiritual Warfare

M ore things on this natural plane are manifested because of prayer than most people can possibly imagine. Learning how to tap into the spiritual world in order to change circumstances in the natural world is indeed the most fascinating experience for which a person can ever hope. Yes, prayer is where the action is. If you can get to the place where you live between amen and here it is, then you have reached a glorious plateau. Upon entering God's rest, you experience peace of mind. You will find that your worries are few, and you are happy and joyful most of the time. God's Word is buried in your heart and in your mind. By learning to trust God, you allow the Holy Spirit to lead you. The realization of your true purpose for being here comes into focus. Regardless of your circumstances, you are continually expecting good things to happen. As a result, God pours out bountiful blessings of love, joy, peace, kindness, and yes, even financial blessings.

If we are not experiencing such blessings in our life, then we have not humbled ourselves before God, and we have not been honest with Him or even with ourselves. To fear the Lord is the beginning of wisdom. This means that we must reverently fear Him; consequently, knowing that, if we do not fear Him, then we will be chastised as any loving father would chastise his children. This type of fear is totally different than having a spirit of fear, which can be crippling. It is very important that we understand the difference in these two types of fear. If we will judge ourselves, then God will not judge us. If we do not judge ourselves, then God will judge us through the Holy Spirit. The result is guilt; we know deep down when we have done something wrong or if we have not obeyed the promptings of the Holy Spirit.

Quick prayers are good when you are in a hurry. However, if many of your prayers are not being answered, then perhaps you are not spending enough time alone with God offering prayers of praise and thanksgiving. Our God is a jealous God, and He loves attention. He loves to be acknowledged and given the glory. Quick prayers are great, though. I cannot tell you the many times that I have misplaced my keys. I have learned to stop and say, "Now Lord, I know that You know where my keys are, and I just want to thank You for showing them to me." Nine times out of ten, He leads me to them within two or three minutes, but He always helps me to find them. The Bible says in *James 4: 2*, *"Ye have not because ye ask not."*

The Bible also says in *Mark 11: 24*, *"What things so ever ye desire when ye pray, believe that ye receive them, and ye shall have them."* In other words, when you pray, if you can come to a place where you honestly believe, without doubt, that what you are asking for is already yours, then you can have whatever you are saying, claiming, and believing. I know this to be true because of the Lord's promise in *John 15: 7: "If ye abide in Me, and My words abide in you, ye shall ask what ye will, and it shall be done unto you."*

According to *John 1: 1*, *"In the beginning was the Word, and the Word was with God, and the Word was God."* God and His Word are one; God is in you to the extent that His Word is in you. When you quote His Word, you bring Him on the scene. However, if you are not continually stretching your faith, then you are gradually slipping back. Then it takes time to get back to where you were before you fell away. The longer you stay away, the harder it is to get back at all. God's Word never changes, but it does change your life. It says in *1*

Peter 1: 23, "The Word of God liveth and abideth forever," and *Hebrews 4: 12* describes God's Word as alive and powerful. God's Word is Living Substance. Learning to rightly divide the Word will produce liberty, power, and strength in your life. Effective prayer destroys the kingdom of darkness and releases the ability of God on earth.

James 1: 6-8 instructs, *"But let him ask in faith, nothing wavering. For he that wavereth is like a wave of the sea driven with the wind and tossed; let not that man think that he shall receive any thing of the Lord. A double minded man is unstable in all his ways."* The name of Jesus, especially proclaimed in prayer, sets up vibrations in the air that release peace all around us. That name has been given to us to control the forces of evil. Most people do not realize the miraculous power released by speaking the name of Jesus. They must be told; it is up to you and me. I know that people today are hungering and thirsting for God more than they ever have. I want so badly for everyone to truly experience God to the extent that I have learned to experience Him. If I seem to tell you the same thing more than once or even twice, it is because repetition is the mother of learning. This book is full of golden nuggets of Truth that I have discovered during the past twenty years. Please pay close attention to what I am about to say.

God says that when you seek Him with all your heart, then you will find Him. You and I can enter into another dimension which goes directly to the throne room of God. God tells us to come boldly to the throne of grace. How do you enter the dimension that leads to God's throne? You can enter through the following steps:

1) Invite Jesus into your heart to be your Lord and Savior; if you have not done so, stop now and ask Him in.

2) Repent of all your sin with a contrite, sincere, and humble spirit.

3) Ask God to help you forgive everyone who has ever hurt you.

4) Praise God and thank Him for all that He has ever done for you.

5) Allow God to wash away your guilt and shame.

If you have taken all these steps and you continue to stay on this straight and narrow path, then you will begin to automatically spend more time alone with God in prayers of praise and worship. You will learn that God inhabits the praises of His people.

Prayer warriors have learned that they have been given spiritual authority over the enemy, Satan. They have learned how to use the Keys of the Kingdom of Heaven. Jesus said in *Matthew 16: 19, "Whatsoever thou shalt bind on earth shall be bound in Heaven."* Therefore, when you come into intercessory prayer, either alone or with someone else, you are able to use the keys that God has given you under a special anointing. The more fervently you pray the stronger the anointing comes upon you and those around you. When you begin to tap into the spiritual world, learning to move the hand of God in a given situation, you will become a prayer warrior. You literally will become addicted to prayer because you will begin to understand that this is where the battles are fought and won. However, you need to have on the full armor of God before you enter the battleground. I want to make it clear now what I meant by moving the hand of God. Some people might misconstrue that whole statement.

You cannot manipulate God and get Him to do everything you want Him to do for you. However, His Word says in *James 5: 16* that *"The effectual, fervent prayer of a righteous man availeth much."* Fervent means a devoted, warm, sincere feeling and to avail means to benefit. You are not righteous in your own strength. You are righteous if Jesus lives in your heart and if you are daily seeking His guidance. If you are a born-again Christian, you have been given the right, according to *Hebrews 4:16,* to *"come boldly unto the throne of grace with prayers of praise and thanksgiving and to make your requests known to God,"* fully expecting answered prayers. If you are not fully expecting good things to happen, then you are not exercising faith. In the midst of many tragic and adverse situations, many people have slipped away and lost themselves in prayers of intercession for someone that they loved. God heard those prayers, and those situations turned around supernaturally because God is the One Who holds all the supernatural power. You can tap into the supernatural power of God, but there are certain requirements:

1) You must believe that God has all the supernatural power and that you can tap into it.
2) You must have only the good of all people in your heart.
3) There can be no selfish motives involved.
4) You must be cleansed and purged of your sins or unforgiveness.
5) You must be able to keep your eyes on Jesus despite the problem, and refrain from talking the problem. Keep your praying and your saying the same.

6) You must keep God's Words hidden in your heart and be ready to quote His promises in the middle of adverse situations.

7) You must never give in to the fear of a situation getting worse.

Faith is the element that makes prayer work. Faith works by love. Faith is what moves God, not prayer alone. I must stress again the importance of keeping your praying and saying the same. If you are praying one thing and saying another, then you are being double minded. Remember, the Bible says in the book of *James, "let not that man ask anything of God."* Praying one thing and saying something contradictory cancels out the faith which you applied in the prayer. Pray believing that God will answer your prayer; do not let the devil talk you into speaking negatively concerning the situation after you finish praying. Stand firmly, no matter what anyone around you is saying.

Prayer is the legal right to ask God to intervene supernaturally on your behalf. It is an aligning of yourself with the Word of God and placing yourself in a position to give God liberty to move on your behalf. Wrong words in prayer will hold you in bondage. They can loose the ability of the enemy against you. Right words will release the ability of God. A prayer accurately formed and stated from God's Word will absolutely move heaven and earth and the things under the earth in your behalf. It is true that God looks upon the heart, and what you have in your heart is what matters. This is where it all must begin. Out of the abundance of the heart, the mouth speaks. What you have in your heart will show in your words and actions.

Another key to answered prayer is speaking words that are in agreement with your daily prayers. Learn to control the words that come out of your mouth. Learn to be patient. *Hebrews 10: 36* proclaims, *"For ye have need of patience, that, after ye have done the will of God, ye might receive the promise."* God's Word is His will for your life and for mine. You must get your mouth into agreement with your mind in order to walk in God's perfect will for your life. Patience undergirds your faith and keeps you steadfast. Yes, prayer is where the action is. If you make a habit of sincere prayer, your life will be naturally and profoundly altered.

Prayer gives you access to the operation of a Supreme Mind and Spirit and releases a spiritual force which shatters fixed states of mind that may have caused many problems for you. The energy and the power released in prayer help you to break through the negative thought strata that previously bound you to all kinds of problems. The impossible becomes possible, and miracles occur. Then you realize that prayer overcame the usual laws of nature and accomplished what others said was impossible. Prayer gives you a sense of peace and tranquility that are attracting powers. Prayer makes you irresistible to your good. It also helps you to change your thinking, which in turn changes your world. Praying releases God's energy within you and around you, an energy that produces right attitudes, reactions, and results in your life.

Ephesians 6: 12 tells us that *"We wrestle not against flesh and blood, but against principalities, against powers, against the rulers of the darkness of this world, against spiritual wickedness in high places."* We may not recognize it, but each of us is in a spiritual battle everyday. Only the people who come to understand this and learn how to overcome it by the grace of God, taking complete and full authority over Satan and his kingdom, will be able to experience true peace that passes all understanding. The ones who have come to this knowledge in God realize that nothing ever can separate them from the love of God. You must be willing to spend time in prayer to make worthwhile changes in your life, in the lives of your loved ones, and in your community and the world. It all starts with you and with me; each must do his part. Praying together is extremely powerful. I think that this is one of the primary reasons that believers should not forsake the gathering of themselves together (attending church). The Bible confirms this. If one can put ten thousand evil spirits to flight, think how many spirits could be made to flee when people join together in prayer. Do you think perhaps our priorities are in the wrong places? We are all trying to fight all the battles independently, but by joining together, we can accomplish more good for each other and for the Kingdom of God.

Jesus said in *John 10: 10, "I am come that they might have life, and that they might have it more abundantly."* He also says to lose your life for His sake so that you might find it. I believe this means that Jesus intends for each person to take everything to the Lord in prayer, dying daily to the flesh and to the cares of this world. This is what Paul meant when he said, *"I die a thousand deaths."*

In *Psalms 34: 1* the Psalmist said, *"I will bless the Lord at all times: His praise shall continually be in my mouth."* I have found that if I center my thoughts on Christ daily, then I experience more joy, inner and outer peace, love, and just general feelings of well-being. However, if I allow my thoughts to roam too far away from Christ, then problems, stress, and confusion seem to bombard me. Blessings come when the peace of God rules in the heart. Jesus is the Prince of Peace. *Isaiah 26: 3* says, *"Thou will keep him in perfect peace, whose mind is stayed on Thee..."* Jesus says in *Matthew 11: 30, "For My yoke is easy, and My burden is light."* Satan is the one who always tries to make life seem difficult and tries to make us suspicious of others. Praise God though, for His wonderful mercy which gives us authority over the works of Satan. Claim the promise of *Matthew 18: 18: "Whatsoever things ye shall bind on earth shall be bound in heaven..."* This is the key to the Kingdom of God. Read it over many times. If you fail to understand how to use this key, then ask God repeatedly until you have no doubt in your mind.

A praying person is given the authority to bind the works of the devil and to cast him into the sea. You can then loose God's wonderful blessings upon the people for whom you are praying. You can authoritatively do this through prayer, and watch God move on their behalf. Speak the words out loud. Remind God what His Word says; He likes to be reminded. He does not forget what He said, but He likes to know that you are aware of what He has instructed you to do. You must never use this law of God for anything other than good. The welfare of all parties should be first and foremost in your mind and actions. I have found that the more I pray for others, the more I am blessed.

Each person has struggles of the flesh against the spirit, and Satan uses every imaginable temptation of the flesh to try to keep us from spending time with the Lord or from spending time doing the Lord's work to promote His kingdom. Satan does not like it when we recognize what he is doing. His goal is to steal, to kill, and to destroy. He will use every effort to steal the Word of God from your heart in an effort to promote negative thinking. One of his best tricks is to try to convince a Christian that he has never been saved. He tries in many ways to bring our past to light in order to make us feel guilty. That is why many Christians backslide; however, either you believe Satan, or you believe what God said about the matter in the Bible. Confessing Jesus Christ as your personal Lord and Savior and being truly repentant before Him assures you of your salvation through Him. You have God's Word on the matter. You must stand boldly on the Word of God and remind Satan of this truth. God gives you authority over Satan if you have been born again. Believing you have that authority and exercising that authority will make it work for you. You must believe in the power of Jesus' name. You are no longer under the law; you are now under God's grace. You will begin to develop a Christ consciousness. You will begin to be able to discern evil spirits easily and see how they work, thus turning to the Lord more often for protection, guidance, and wisdom. The blood of Jesus needs to be applied through daily prayer to every circumstance in your life, your family's life, and to a lost and dying world.

Ephesians 4: 22-24 tells us to *"Put off our old self, which is being corrupted by its deceitful desires, to be made anew in the attitude of our minds, and to put on the new self, created to be like God in true righteousness and holiness."* The battle begins in the mind. It is true that we cannot control every thought, evil or good, but we can choose to rebuke certain thoughts in the name of Jesus. Satan has a field day when he is successful at sending us an evil or a negative thought, and we entertain it in our minds. If a person plays with an evil thought long enough, then his actions usually will follow through in time. Negative actions follow negative thoughts. Be assured that loving words and actions follow loving thoughts. You can win the war which starts in your mind with the power of Jesus, and nothing but the blood of Jesus can set you free. He is, indeed, The Way, The Truth, and The Life.

Psalms 97: 10-11 reads, *"Let those who love the Lord hate evil, for He guards the lives of His faithful ones and delivers them from the hand of the wicked. Light is shed upon righteousness, and joy on the upright of heart."* Certain conditions for victory over Satan must be met. Jesus commands in *Mark 11: 22, "Have faith in God."* In *Revelation 12: 11* John speaks of the atoning power of Jesus' blood. *Luke 10: 19* promises the believer a power that can overcome evil. *Acts 10: 38* tells believers to trust in the power of the Holy Spirit. All these verses prove that oppression can be broken. Dealing with evil requires the above tools that are available to Christians. It is up to each individual to use these tools.

This country was founded upon Godly principles, and when our government was first formed, there were primarily Godly men in city, state, and federal political positions. I believe that George Washington was a devout Christian, a man of unceasing prayer. God instructs us in His Word to pray unceasingly. What that means is to develop an attitude of gratitude – a God consciousness, understanding that He is at work in other people even when we may think otherwise. A Christian is a person who has declared Jesus as his Lord and Savior, who believes that Jesus died on the cross for his sins, and who strives to live a life that is pleasing in God's sight. Being a Christian does not bring perfection; human beings will never be perfect. Jesus is the only perfect One. Be reminded that Buddha, Mohammed nor Hare Krishna died on a cross for us; only Jesus Christ Who was God Himself manifested in the flesh.

Most of us live in respect of the law; however, there are universal laws of God far more powerful than any man-made law. His Word is meant to be used to help us to walk victoriously here on earth. God really does not want to hear words of discouragement. Our praying and our saying must become the same. God's Word is supernaturally more powerful than the human brain intellectually can understand. It can be understood only through the Holy Spirit after one accepts Jesus as Lord and Savior. Each person is engaged in a spiritual battle. The forces of darkness are very real, but God is always there to welcome you with open, loving arms when you turn to Him.

Hebrews 11: 1 says, *"Now faith is the substance of things hoped for, the evidence of things not seen."* Faith should be applied at all times, especially when things seem bleak. It is easy to exhibit faith when life is running smoothly. We are constantly speaking words of fear and doubt or words full of faith, and the people who hear those words know where we are in our walk with the Lord. We believe our own words far more quickly than the words of others, so doesn't it make sense that we should be careful of our words? Speaking out loud God's loving and encouraging words for yourself or for others builds the mountain-moving faith that we all want. When everything around you looks gloomy and hopeless, then that is the time to put on the full armor of God. Stand firmly on God's Word, fully expecting God to reveal His glory to you. This is applied faith; however, faith without works is dead. You must work the Word, and it will work for you. This is the only way you can effectively quench the fiery darts of the wicked. You must be very careful what you wish for other people. Negative thoughts have only an adverse effect, and they are usually like a boomerang.

Sometimes though, visible changes may be hard to detect in a person who has been born again. However, a born-again Christian knows in his heart that he is not the same. The value of salvation is different for everyone. How valuable it is to each person determines how closely that person will walk with the Lord from then on. Each person has choices about how closely he wants to work with the Holy Spirit everyday of his life. God works with different people in different ways. He never forces Himself on anyone. He is always there, gently nudging us to draw closer to Him, to trust Him, and to let Him love us, but we have to want to accept His love. Only acceptance of His love enables us to give unconditional love to others.

When you make your requests known to God through prayers of praise and thanksgiving, He will hear you. When you fall deeply in love with Jesus, sometimes you just want to praise Him and worship Him without asking for anything. God loves this; He inhabits the praises of His people. It is in praising Him that His precious, anointing grace comes upon you full force. That is why it is called Amazing Grace. God's grace is nothing to fear. It is true that the fear of the Lord is the beginning of wisdom, but you have learned how to reverently fear the Lord by choosing to be quick to repent, thus allowing God's precious, anointing Holy Spirit to fall upon you. When you can learn to forget what others are doing and choose to enter into full praise and worship, you will develop a powerful thirst to do this more often because of the wonderful peace and love you will experience. Such praise and worship is to truly experience God; this is the ultimate here on earth! However, it may be quite difficult to do this unless you first start doing it in your private time with God. Just lift your arms to the Lord at home and start praising Him sometime. This act is Biblical and it is an act of surrender. God loves it when he looks down and sees His children surrendering to Him, as if we are wanting Him to pick us up and put us in His lap. God loves you. Let Him love you more fully and completely.

If you do not receive answers to your prayers, then something is wrong. Perhaps you have disobeyed God. You know deep down in your heart when you have disobeyed God and have not asked for forgiveness. I cannot stress enough how important it is to be daily purged and cleansed from sin. As the old hymn reminds us, "How precious is the flow that washes white as snow; no other fount I know, nothing but the blood of Jesus." Only the knowledge of His saving grace can wash away the guilt when we have sinned. Knowledge, however, is worth nothing alone. Knowledge is power only when it is applied. If you have gossiped, have treated anyone unkind in any way, or have thought an unkind thought about anyone, then take these sins to the cross daily. God is always ready to hear your prayers and your requests.

I am not saying that you will always get everything for which you pray. God knows exactly what you need and when you need it much better than you do. God is never too early nor too late with His answers; His timing is perfect. God knows you are not perfect, but He is looking for those who will trust and obey His voice and spend time with Him and in His Word so that His kingdom will be promoted and so that others will be brought into His full grace. God created you for His pleasure, not for your own pleasure. When you are willing to obey Him and all His laws and commands, then He is willing to pour out abundant blessings on you. He owns everything, and there is an abundance of everything.

There is no short supply of anything unless you believe there is.

When we are in deep, fervent prayers of praise and we invite the Holy Spirit in, we can feel the precious anointing of the Holy Spirit. Faith and trust in God rush in, and our words become very powerful under that anointing. In *2 Corinthians 4: 13* we are reminded to learn to speak what God says and not what we think. Words spoken under that anointing must be full of love and compassion for God and all mankind. When they are, little miracles begin to happen, and then bigger ones happen. Then you find yourself addicted to prayer. That is where the action is!

Reference to the anointing of the Holy Spirit is found in *1 John 2: 27: "But the anointing which ye have received of Him abideth in you, and ye need not that any man teach you anything: but as the same anointing teacheth you of all things, and is truth, and is no lie, and even as it hath taught you, ye shall abide in Him."* Only prayer keeps the anointing power of the Holy Spirit upon you. God says that you are to pray unceasingly. You may not be able to pray openly all the time, but you can pray silently far more often that you are doing it right now. You need to stay in prayer to keep the anointing factor working for you. This keeps you in an attitude of gratitude. The more grateful you are, the more God will continue to bless you. The pressures of this world, involving money, desires of the flesh, or the cares of this world, tend to affect our minds. The tactics of Satan are sometimes subtle, and unless we are staying in close communion with the Lord and daily confessing our sins, then we can easily lose God's anointing grace. Sin separates us from God. If we are not willing to let go of a sin, we tend to avoid prayer altogether, thus discouraging any conversation concerning God or spiritual matters. The yoke of bondage can be broken by confessing our sins. Confession is good for the soul (mind, will, emotions).

We need to learn to separate the problem from the pressure. When dealing with the pressure, if we learn to understand why it is there and take it to the cross, then the problem will take care of itself. God does not want to hear us talk problems; He already knows when there is a problem. He wants us to have more faith and trust in Him. He wants to hear that we are standing firmly on His Word, quoting His covenant promises. This causes Satan to flee. Rehearsing a problem over and over will keep the problem there. Hope comes from God's covenant of promises, and hope is the anchor of the soul. If you start feeling that problems will not work out, then hope has no anchor. Feelings do not really matter; they change. God's Word does not change. Neither does He. He is the same yesterday, today, and tomorrow. You can learn to fully expect God's covenant promises to happen in your life, but study and sacrifice are necessary. If we choose a blessed way of life, then we are chastised by God until we are ready.

Those who are blessed possess the keys to God's storehouse. The keys are:

1) Forgiveness and restoration

2) Healing

3) Prosperity and productivity

4) Angelic assistance

5) Creativity

6) God's strategy

All of these keys are available to those who choose the blessed way of life. As Jesus said in *Matthew 11: 30, "My yoke is easy, and My burden is light."* Believe it; it is true!

Churches today need to create an atmosphere of worship in order for the anointing to flow. People are missing out on the blessings because of the lack of anointing. The Bible says that the traditions of men are what hold them back. The majority of the traditional churches today are suffering from a lack of the anointing because they are so adamant about doing things the same old way. Well, God is doing a new thing today. Church services cannot continue to be so ritualistic and expect to receive the full blessings of grace, peace, and joy. God's people must wander out a little deeper into the Living Water. People are hungering to be in the presence of God. The presence of the Holy Spirit must be invited into the church; He must be made to feel welcome. He will not come in where He is not made to feel completely welcome. The presence of the Holy Spirit can be ushered into a sanctuary during songs of praise and worship. This should not be hurried. This is where God is experienced in His full Glory. Churches need to drop their fear of offending their congregations. When the leaders of the church drop this fear, then the congregation will follow suit. Churches need to let *Hebrews 10:19* become their driving force: *"Having therefore, brethren, boldness to enter into the holiest by the blood of Jesus."*

God's people should not offend the majesty of God by trying to bring Him to their regular mindset. The pure power of God is accessible. His people must make the choice to access that power. We need to learn to praise God much more deeply because there is probably an eternal worship service going on in heaven, and we need the practice. God's people can touch the hem of His garment if they want to badly enough. *Revelation 3: 13 and Revelation 3: 22* say, *"HE THAT HATH AN EAR, LET HIM HEAR WHAT THE SPIRIT SAITH UNTO THE CHURCHES."* Do you suppose that this must be important for God to repeat the exact same words in the same chapter of the same book of the Bible?

To connect with God, we need the anointing. We can get the anointing only by prayer and praise. We need to become less self-conscious and more God-conscious. We must decrease. He must increase within us. Christ in you is the hope of glory is what His Word says. If God's glory is to shine throughout all the world it must shine through all His children. There has been enough theology and enough debate. Nothing excites the heart of God more than His people worshipping Him. If you have received Jesus as your personal Lord and Savior, then you have received diplomatic immunity, and you cannot be prosecuted by Satan. You must participate. *Hebrews 2: 12* says, *"I will declare Thy name unto my brethren, in the midst of the church will I sing praise unto Thee."*

The throne room of God is available. You can create a vacuum by emptying yourself. By losing consciousness of self and extending your arms to God, you will experience an overflow of His precious love, peace, and grace. The extended hand is a symbol of thanksgiving. Forget tradition.

Forget someone standing next to you. Do you want to be blessed, or do you want to try to make sure that everyone thinks you are prim and proper? What value does that hold? You can be prim and proper later. For now, worship God the way He wants to be worshipped in corporate prayers of praise and thanksgiving. You will receive bountiful blessings! If all this sounds too emotional, then perhaps it is, but the only way to experience God is through the emotions. It is easy to lose God's anointing grace unless you have become Christ-conscious. Encountering the negativity of daily life tends to grate on the spirit, wearing it down. In order for the Living Water to be stirred up again, we must come back to the cross and back to Jesus, the living Water. *John 7: 37* tells us that, *"In the last day, that great day of the feast, Jesus stood and cried, saying, 'If any man thirst, let him come unto Me, and drink.'"*

An arsenal of spiritual weapons is available to the believer! The following verses tell of the power available to Christians through the name of Jesus and His shed blood:

Psalms 44:5: "Through Thee will we push down our enemies: through Thy name will we tread them under that rise up against us."

Mark 16: 17: "And these signs shall follow them that believe; In My name shall they cast out devils; they shall speak with new tongues."

Luke 9: 1-2: "Then He called His twelve disciples together, and gave them power and authority over all devils, and to cure diseases. And He sent them to preach the kingdom of God, and to heal the sick."

John 14: 13-14: "And whatsoever ye shall ask in My name, that will I do, that the Father may be glorified in the Son. If ye shall ask any thing in My name, I will do it."

Philippians 2: 9-10: "Blotting out the handwriting of ordinances that was against us, which was contrary to us, and took it out of the way, nailing it to His cross; And having spoiled principalities and powers, He made a shew of them openly, triumphing over them in it."

We must pull down every stronghold, taking captive any and every thought that tries to assert itself against the Kingdom of God and cast down every evil imagination. TAKE CONTROL OF YOUR THOUGHTS!!!!!! If we are dwelling on the flaws in other people, then we are limiting ourselves of living a truly blessed life here on this earth. We need to be quick to forgive and love other people regardless of how they may treat us.

Prayer in Jesus' name is a powerful spiritual weapon available to those who have accepted Christ as Lord and Savior. When we Christians unite in His name, humbling ourselves before Him, we can and will make a difference in this world, and God will heal our land as He promised.

Chapter Eight

Spiritual Gifts From God

Holiness is what we must seek first and foremost. This comes from seeking the glory of God. Our goals should not be to just become powerful; we can do nothing without the anointing of the Holy Spirit; at least nothing worthwhile and everlasting. *John 5: 44* asks, *"How can ye believe, which receive honour one of another, and seek not the honour that cometh from God only?"* When we truly want God and His glory, then our hunger for Him will cause us to forsake the praise from other people. One way that God's glory is manifested to us is through the spiritual gifts that He gives to believers. In *1 Corinthians 12: 1* we read, *"Now concerning spiritual gifts, brethren, I would not have you ignorant."* God wants us to know about and to understand these gifts and to receive these gifts from Him. We cannot receive them if we don't take the time to know what they are and how they should be used in the Kingdom of God. According to *1 Corinthians 12: 4-7, "Now there are diversities of gifts, but the same Spirit. And there are differences of administrations, but the same Lord. And there are diversities of operations, but it is the same God which worketh all in all. But the manifestation of the Spirit is given to every man to profit withal."* The word profit means to get advantage, to gain, or to benefit. I think it would be safe to say that we are all seeking to gain or to benefit, or to get advantage, wouldn't you? Therefore, let's study these gifts and start using them so that we can profit in the Kingdom of God.

The spiritual gifts that God gives us are discussed in the twelfth chapter of *1 Corinthians,* verses eight through fourteen:

"For to one is given by the Spirit the word of wisdom; to another the word of knowledge by the same Spirit; To another faith by the same Spirit; to another the gifts of healing by the same Spirit; To another the working of miracles; to another prophecy; to another discerning of spirits; to another divers kinds of tongues; to another the interpretation of tongues: But all these worketh that

*one and the selfsame Spirit, dividing to every man sever-
ally as he will. For as the body is one, and hath many
members, and all the members of that one body, being
many, are one body; so also is Christ. For by one Spirit
are we all baptized into one body, whether we be Jews
or Gentiles, whether we be bond or free; and have been
all made to drink into one Spirit. For the body is not one
member, but many."*

It is my opinion that God would like for us to have as
many of these gifts as we are able to receive. Receiving is
the key word here. To receive them, we must know about
them, understand how they work and for what purpose, and
then pray to receive them. These gifts are very precious, and
they do serve an important, divine purpose. They are not
arbitrarily poured out from God on just anybody and everybody. God does not have any favorites, but He does have
many imtimates. A person must first desire to have something before he or she can receive it. I know you agree with
that, right? God said that if we would delight ourselves in
Him that He would give us the desires of our hearts. If the
desire to have a certain spiritual gift has been planted in your
heart, then it is there for a purpose. It is up to you to stay in
prayer, seeking God, and asking Him to reveal how, where,

and when this gift is to be used. Let's look at the different gifts and try to understand their purpose.

The gift of the *word of wisdom* is a gift of supernatural revelation of divine purpose with God's voice coming through an individual. This gift is not learned. A person with this gift is full of the Holy Spirit, and the Spirit of God is speaking through him or her. The word of wisdom speaks about future events and calls for action revealing the purpose and will of God.

The *word of knowledge* is given to reveal the enemy's plan of destruction, to enlighten and encourage, and to set the captive free. When the word of knowledge is spoken, faith rises and miracles happen!

The *discerning of spirits* reveals the kind of spirit that is motivating a person at the time the manifestation is taking place and is used to help deliver the afflicted, tormented, and oppressed. This is done with a pure spirit of love and has nothing to do with psychic powers or anything of that kind. This has to do with the development of the human powers of judgment. It is not psychological insight.

The gifts of *healings, miracles, and faith* are the power gifts. Sickness and disease are not from God. He does not put these afflictions on us to teach us anything. It is not His will for us to be sick. We must be able to receive a healing from God. This healing sometimes comes divinely, or it can be a process. Miracles happen only when there is no natural means of man to accomplish anything. Eighty-five percent of the healings are received as a process. Angelic assistance is usually a part of the miracles that happens. Faith is the substance of things hoped for and the evidence of things not seen. We all have different levels of faith. We can either have positive faith, which is used to believe God for something good, or we can have negative faith, believing that something dreadful is going to happen. Negative faith is, of course, fear.

The gift of *prophecy* has to do with edification, which is the act of building up and promoting spiritual growth. Exhortation is a part of prophecy in the sense that someone is urged to pursue some course of conduct. There is a degree of comfort being given having to do with the trial experienced. There must be a calling from God to prophesy, or else a person could cause division in the church.

The fourteenth chapter of *1 Corinthians* tells us of the gifts of *tongues and interpretation of tongues.* In verses four and five we read, *"He that speaketh in an unknown tongue edifieth himself; but he that prophesieth edifieth the church. I would that ye all spake with tongues, but rather that ye prophesied: for greater is he that prophesieth than he that speaketh with tongues, except he interpret, that the church may receive edifying.* " In this same chapter, verses 27 and 28 tell us, *"If any man speak in an unknown tongue, let it be by two, or at the most by three, and that by course; and let one interpret. But if there be no interpreter, let him keep silence in the church; and let him speak to himself, and to God. "*

I was raised in a traditional Methodist church where these gifts were surely preached from the pulpit, but I sure don't remember them being preached at all. When I was in high school, we lived across the street from a big, old, white building. I think it had been at one time a feed storage building. I remember early one evening when a couple of my girlfriends and I were roaming around. Naturally curious, we wandered around behind that building because we heard the music coming from inside. We thought somebody must be having a really wild party inside. Once we got close enough we realized that it was what we called back then a "holy roller" church. They were playing drums, singing, shouting, and just really having church. However, this was totally for- eign to us, so fear of the unknown reared its ugly head. We tend not to believe in anything in which we are not familiar. There is usually an element of fear involved. We sure didn't act that way in our church. As you can imagine, all kinds of thoughts popped into our heads. Were these people crazy? Did they belong to a cult? Since then, things have changed dramatically. After I received the baptism of the Holy Spirit in October of 1987, the blinders were lifted from my eyes. I started attending Mt. Paran Church of God church in Atlanta, Georgia. I loved going there, and I began to lift my hands to the Lord as they were doing. I absolutely loved the freedom of not having to worry about what others would think because they were all, or mostly all, raising their hands, too. However, occasionally someone would speak in another tongue, and this bothered me. It made me fearful for a while. Then I began to pray and ask God to reveal to me why they did that. If you want to know something, just ask God. We have not because we ask not. I read a book of Benny Hinn's entitled *Good Morning Holy Spirit*. This book opened my eyes to a lot of truth. The Holy Spirit is magnificent. He will reveal things to us as we are ready to receive them. Praise God; He is truly awesome in the way He works.

I began to pray for the gift of tongues, but it did not come easily. My intellectual mind kept getting in the way, telling me this was stupid and had no purpose. I soon discovered that this was Satan trying to keep me from growing to another level in Christ. He didn't win. I finally received the gift of tongues. Let me attempt to share with you what this gift has meant to me. After I had learned how powerful prayer is and how much God truly loves me, I also realized that Satan kept trying to keep me from spending time alone with God, and he really tried to keep me from praying. I'm on to his dumb tricks now. However, after a while we really don't know about what we should pray. God already knows the problem. He doesn't want us reciting the problem to Him. He wants us to grow closer to Him and let His pure love flow into us, through us, and out of us. If a person desires the gift of speaking in tongues, there is a place that he or she can come to, where, after praying, he or she can be so lost in the love of God that the Spirit will take over and make intercession for him. This is the gift of tongues. You will always feel a deep sense of peace, grace, and joy afterwards. All tension is relieved and discarded. You can also pray for the interpretation of the heavenly language that God has given to you. Many people believe that the gift of speaking in tongues automatically comes when you are baptized in the Holy Spirit. It didn't happen that way for me. It was two years later and I had to pray to receive that gift.

Yes, the gifts of God are wonderful. He wants us to have them. Desiring to have them is key. He wants us to use them to help us to walk in victory here on earth and to bring others into the full grace of our Lord and Savior, Jesus Christ. He is King of Kings and Lord of Lords. He deserves all the praise, honor, and glory. God deserves for us to hold our hands up in full surrender to Him. He deserves to be praised and worshipped. He deserves to be consulted about our day and what to do with it. He deserves to be put first in everything that we do. He deserves our full participation in seeking to live a godly life, one that is pleasing in His sight. He is the only way to find true peace, happiness, joy, love, and grace. Jesus is the Way, the Truth, and the Life.

People are always saying they are seeking truth. Many don't realize it, but they need Jesus, the only One Who can ever or will ever fill the void in the human heart. That's just the way we were created. There is no other way to get to God or to enter the Kingdom of God. Jesus is the secretary, if you want to look at it that way. Jesus is the only One that satisfies. We hunger and thirst for a relationship with Him. It is one thing to know that Jesus loves us. It is indeed another thing to learn to forgive ourselves. We *cannot* forgive ourselves without a close, personal relationship with Jesus. If we cannot forgive ourselves and learn to fully embrace the love of Christ, then how can we possibly truly love others? I am not going to try to pretend that I have a wealth of knowledge about all the spiritual gifts from God because I am still in a major learning mode where this is concerned. However, there is a wealth of information concerning these spiritual gifts. They are all outlined in the Bible, of course, and there are numerous books available that I am quite sure can help to enlighten a person on these topics.

Let's talk about healing in a little more detail. So many thousands of people are interested in this subject. God is a good God; healing is His will. His very nature is to heal. From the beginning to the end, the Bible makes it clear that it has always been God's will to heal His people. There are many promises of God's healing outlined in the Bible. The following are just a few of these promises:

Exodus 23: 25: "And ye shall serve the Lord your God, and He shall bless thy bread, and thy water; and I will take sickness away from the midst of thee."

Psalms 34: 19: "Many are the afflictions of the righteous: but the Lord delivereth him out of them all."

Psalms 103: 1-5: "Bless the Lord, O my soul: and all that is within me, bless His holy name. Bless the Lord, O my soul, and forget not all His benefits: Who forgiveth all thine iniquities; Who healeth all thy diseases; Who redeemeth thy life from destruction; Who crowneth thee with lovingkindness and tender mercies; Who satisfieth thy mouth with good things; so that thy youth is renewed like the eagle's."

Psalms 107: 19-21: *"Then they cry unto the Lord in their trouble, and He saveth them out of their distresses. He sent His Word, and healed them, and delivered them from their destructions. Oh that men would praise the Lord for His goodness, and for His wonderful works to the children of men!"*

Isaiah 41: 10: *"Fear thou not; for I am with thee: be not dismayed; for I am thy God: I will strengthen thee; yea, I will help thee; yea I will uphold thee with the right hand of my righteousness."*

Jeremiah 30: 17: *"For I will restore health unto thee, and I will heal thee of thy wounds, saith the Lord; because they called thee an Outcast, saying, This is Zion, whom no man seeketh after."*

Malachi 4: 2: *"But unto you that fear My name shall the Son of righteousness arise with healing in His wings; and ye shall go forth and grow up as calves of the stall."*

Healing is more than God's will. It is His provision. The price for your healing was paid at Calvary; it is part of your redemption. The following verses illustrate this point:

John 10:10: "The thief cometh not, but for to steal, and to kill, and to destroy: I am come that they might have life, and that they might have it more abundantly."

Isaiah 53: 4-5: "Surely He hath borne our griefs, and carried our sorrows: yet we did esteem Him stricken, smitten of God, and afflicted. But He was wounded for our transgressions, He was bruised for our iniquities: the chastisement of our peace was upon Him; and with His stripes we are healed."

1 Peter 2: 24: "Who His own self bare our sins in His own body on the tree, that we, being dead to sins, should live unto righteousness: by Whose stripes ye were healed."

Isaiah 54: 17: "No weapon that is formed against thee shall prosper; and every tongue that shall rise against thee in judgment thou shalt condemn. This is the heritage of the servants of the Lord, and their righteousness is of Me, saith the Lord."

Galatians 3: 13-14, 29: "Christ hath redeemed us from the curse of the law, being made a curse for us: for it is written, Cursed is every one that hangeth on a tree: That the blessing of Abraham might come on the Gentiles through Jesus Christ; that we might receive the promise of the Spirit through the faith. And if ye be Christ's, then are ye Abraham's seed, and heirs according to the promise."

Jesus revealed God's will as He continually ministered healing and deliverance during His time on Earth. Jesus is still the healer. *Matthew*, chapter nine, talks about Jesus healing the eyes of two blind men. He told them that it would be done unto them according to their faith. The same chapter tells of the woman who had an issue of blood for twelve years; she just wanted to touch the hem of Jesus' garment. He told her that her faith had made her whole from that hour. The following Scriptures are just a few of the many that enlighten us about Jesus' healing ministry:

Matthew 12: 22: "Then was brought unto Him one possessed with a devil, blind, and dumb: and he healed him, insomuch that the blind and dumb both spake and saw."

Matthew 14: 14: "And Jesus went forth, and saw a great multitude, and was moved with compassion toward them, and He healed their sick."

Matthew 21: 14: "And the blind and the lame came to Him in the temple; and He healed them."

Chapter seventeen in the book of *Luke* tells of ten lepers. Jesus told them to go show themselves to the priests, and as they went, they were cleansed. One of them, after seeing that he was healed, looked back, fell down, and started praising God. Jesus said, *"Go, thy faith hath made thee whole."* The fifth chapter of *John* talks of a man who had an infirmity for thirty-eight years. Jesus asked him if he wanted to be made whole, and He told the man to take up his bed and walk. The man exercised his faith by obeying Jesus, and he was made whole.

When Jesus sent His disciples to preach the good news, He also commissioned them to heal the sick. He told them in *John 14: 12, "Verily, verily, I say unto you, He that believeth on Me, the works that I do shall he do also; and greater works than these shall he do; because I go unto My Father."* Healing is your right as a born-again child of God. Throughout the New Testament, God reminds us of that inheritance and exhorts us to live in the fullness of it. Chapter five in the book of *James* tells us that if there are any sick among us to call for the elders of the church to anoint and pray for those sick, thus bringing about the saving and healing of the sick. Even though healing is God's unchangeable will for you, it does not come automatically. You must receive it just as you received your new birth, by faith in God's Word. We must stand in faith, believing God. If you have faith in your heart and God's Word in your mouth, healing will come. It may take time for it to manifest in your body, so stand fast in faith, giving thanks to God until it does. Focus on God and His Word, not on physical symptoms. We must seek first the Kingdom of God and His righteousness and all things will be added unto us (*Matthew 6: 33*).

I personally know that this is not easy to do since I have experienced numerous health challenges these last few years. I am sixty-five years of age as of the release of this book and have always been very healthy, or so I thought up until 1996. I had always taken vitamin supplements, at least 1000 mg of Vitamin C, and a B-complex every day for over fifteen years. I stopped taking them and within six months, my immune system obviously collapsed. I now also know that one of my thirty year old silicone implants ruptured. It would take fives years to realize this. I learned the hard way that it is detrimental to your health to come off Vitamin C suddenly. I became sick with six health problems all at once: flu, pneumonia, hepatitis B, shingles, overactive parathyroid, and hormonal imbalance. I prayed almost every waking moment, I felt like the devil was definitely trying to kill me. I felt as if I had been plugged into an electrical outlet for 3 weeks. He didn't succeed, though. I'm still kicking. Within two months time, I had overcome all that the devil had used to try to destroy me, or so I thought. I started a new job selling carpet in a retail store. My marriage was pretty shaky, to say the least, and I left my husband in August of 1996. My stepfather of fourteen years suffered a heart attack and had died at the age of eighty-nine in July. I have three sisters, and there was confusion about what to do with Mother. Two and one-half years in this last marriage was more than enough for me, so I moved in with my Mother, who was eighty-six years old at the time. It took eight months or so to get my nerves back together, and in April of 1997, I accepted a position with a local nursing home as a nurse's aide. Why should I do this, with an eighteen years sales background? There were several reasons:

1. I had been a nurse's aide in high school and had always regretted not pursuing nursing as a career.
2. The hospital that owned the nursing home would reimburse tuition for me to go to school after being employed for a year.
3. The hospital gave in-house transfers, even to clerical positions, etc.
4. I have a lot of compassion in my heart, and I saw this opportunity as a ministry.

Little did I know that I had bitten off almost more than I could chew.

I started having chest pains in June. The wing on which I worked consisted primarily of totally dependent residents. There was always a shortage of help because of the physically demanding nature of the job. We seldom were able to get our thirty-minute lunch break. The residents needed care. When working alone, which was quite often, we would have to hold firmly with one hand the dead weight of the residents on their hips while rolling their soiled pads out from under them so that they could be cleaned and changed. Then we would roll them back over from the other side. I believe this is what started my chest pains, this plus the fact that silicone which contains over forty neurotoxins were flowing through my entire body (I now know, but didn't then). Sometimes when we were able to slip away for thirty minutes, I would go into the quiet room, lie down and relax, and talk to the Lord. The pain would go away. I remember two different occasions when only one other nurse's aide and I had to care for forty-eight residents. On a good day five or six aids were at work. Many of the residents, even the totally dependent ones, had to be helped out of bed every day, bathed or showered, dressed, and put in a wheelchair or gerry chair. Their families expected it, and you can't blame them for that.

About twenty residents had to be fed at every meal. Then we had to put all of them back to bed, stripping them from the waist down for their afternoon rest period. In between, all the linens had to be changed, showers and baths had to be given, urinals and bedpans had to be handed out, and the daily routine had to be noted on their charts.

I loved each and every one of those residents, even the ones who were somewhat, to say the least, less than loveable many times. I prayed with and for many of them, and I loved to see the sparkle in their eyes when I talked to them about Jesus. I loved going with them to the cafeteria once a week to sing the old-time gospel songs along with the others. Bless their hearts; they seemed to enjoy it so much. Unfortunately, for reasons other than I have already mentioned, this was less than an ideal place to work. The majority of the elderly people in that nursing home resented the black people who took care of them, and it was sometimes hard for the aides to take the open, verbal abuse thrown at them. Many of the residents had watched some of the aids going through their personal belongings. Regrettably, this does happen, but some were also falsely accused.

I forced myself to come to work every day with joy in my heart despite the hard working conditions. The first two weeks I came home, got into a tub of warm water, and cried, my heart breaking for all those people and self pity beginning to set in for the physical pain I began to have. I eventually got past the tough emotional impact of the situation; after all, there was much work to be done, over and over and over. It seemed we were never caught up with anything because the needs were so monumental. The video they had shown us in training led me to believe I would have all this time to minister to the emotional and spiritual needs of these people. The truth is that there was only about five percent of our time left over for that after meeting their physical needs. Never before have I ever witnessed in or worked in a place where there was such a strong, spiritual battle going on. Hostility from the residents, their families, the co-workers, and the supervisors was almost constant. Some days seemed peaceful, but they were few and far between. All the aids worked under the threat of being written up for this and that. One of the nurses treated the aids like she was our drill sergeant. Fear intimidation was used to the fullest; trying to care for the residents was hard enough without that. Most of the time I was an open witness for Christ. Rest assured Satan didn't like that. When I was physically exhausted, I slipped out from under grace a few times. Aside from going through the fire in the marriage I had come out of the year before, standing up for Christ and for everything He represents on that job was the hardest thing I have ever had to do.

The nurses kept telling me that my chest pains probably were caused by gall bladder trouble. I finally went to the doctor in August. He started running all kinds of tests, but he never found anything. I believe it was around September when I started having strange muscle pains sporadically. I was diagnosed with osteoporosis on October 13, 1997, my last day at work. I later found out that the isolated, strange, acute pain going from my lower back down my left leg was caused by a ruptured, herniated disk in my lower back. It had happened when I bent over to help a lady put on her shoes. Workman's compensation would not agree to pay for my back surgery until February 20, 1998, so I suffered for four months with that. Around October 23, 1997, ten days after my last day at work, I experienced a deep wave of pain sweeping down from my lower back into my hip area and thighs. I thought if this is osteoporosis, then it is the most horrible thing one could ever imagine. I applied for disability the next day. An MRI on October 30 revealed the ruptured disk. I can't help but believe that the ruptured disk threw me into full-blown fibromyalgia and myofascial pain syndrome. The situation became even worse. I had to suffer with the disk problem for four months before the surgery was done.

All of my body rhythms had been thrown out of sync. The only reason I am going into detail about my health condition is that I hope something I say will shed some light on a situation for someone else. Unfortunately, the medical schools only touch on the subject of the muscles in the human body. Therefore, doctors do not receive the education they need in order to treat their patients appropriately. However, there are people working hard to change this, praise God. The good news is that some of the medical schools are now teaching alternative medicine including nutrition, etc. In the past doctors have received only a few hours education in nutrition. How sad that is when God created our bodies with needs for vitamins and minerals.

Let me describe how I felt for 10 years. When I would get up in the mornings, it took a good hour just to work the stiffness out. I usually had a headache that started in the back of my neck. It sometimes felt like the blood going to my brain was going to be cut off. I usually had another headache in the late afternoon. When I would sit over twenty or thirty minutes, the muscles in my thighs felt like they were setting up like concrete. I had to take frequent rest intervals throughout the day to keep from being completely overcome with fatigue and pain. My concentration level left something to be desired. My short-term memory was affected.

This is called fibrofog. All the fibromites know what I'm talking about. The muscles in my right hand started to ache after using the clicker on the mouse for even just an hour. The muscles throughout my whole body vibrated to varying degrees at all times. They were never at rest totally because the central nervous system is affected, which caused me to get excited or agitated very easily. There were tight bands around my upper thighs which affected the range of motion with my legs. I couldn't walk for a long period of time because the pain in my thighs was overwhelming. These pains were stabbing, shooting, sometimes knife-like pains behind the thighs. Sometimes it was like a knife being twisted. I had some ringing in my ears, frequent heart palpitations, and vision changes from time to time. I experienced shortness of breath. My chiropractor said I was losing cartilage from my bones. That is why they cracked and popped, and it seemed to be getting worse. My hip bones seemed to be losing much range of motion, and my knees sometimes buckled. Insomnia was a major problem, as the REM stage of sleep is almost impossible to reach. This is the stage where the body can heal and restore itself. In addition, diarrhea was a problem for quite some time. While lying on my side with my ear on the pillow, I could feel and hear something moving in both ears. I guess it was muscles vibrating; I don't know. I could see flashes of light when I first woke up every morning. The hamstrings in my thighs were extremely tight because the muscles stayed contracted a lot, unless I did a lot of stretching exercises throughout the day. We were taught to bare the bulk of the weight on our thighs instead of our backs when lifting residents in the nursing home. If I wasn't very careful and didn't rest as much as I should, the chronic fatigue on top of the pain could seem almost unbearable. It could hit me like a freight train.

By the grace of God I have learned the hard way how to manage all of these problems at least to a certain degree. Everything we receive from God is by His hand of grace. I am still learning to cope. I have learned that alternative medicine is the only way to treat these disorders. Actually, nutrition is the ultimate way. Alternative medicine means chiropractors for an adjustment, frequent massages, acupuncture, and nutrition. I have spent a small fortune on this along with herbal supplements because insurance does not cover any of these things. Although I don't put any synthetic drugs into my body, I do not recommend anyone coming off prescribed medicine without first consulting your doctor. Nevertheless, there are alternative medicines, and they have only a fraction of the risks of prescription medicines. You should also know that over 100,000 deaths per year occur because of prescribed drugs. Please understand that I am not against doctors. They are great for emergencies, etc.; they have their place. I just personally do not believe in matching symptoms with drugs. This is my opinion and it is my book. We live in a very toxic environment these days. Since World War II there are more than 76,000 toxic chemicals in the atmosphere according to scientists. It is up to the individual to identify the toxins that may be causing him or her trouble (mine was silicone). As far as I'm concerned, this is the first step. It makes sense to follow this with proper nutrition since we are not born with prescribed chemicals (drugs) in our brains. Never come off a prescribed drug abruptly or without consulting your doctor, please!!!

I have read and studied everything I can get my hands on concerning health and nutrition. I have come to the conclusion, along with other people, that a high percentage of our health problems stems from animal products. We have over 120 hormones in our bodies. Cattle are being injected with hormones so they can be taken to slaughter within two years in order to turn a quicker profit. When we eat that meat, the extra estrogen in that animal is causing our estrogen to go entirely out of balance. The same goes for chicken. In addition, our digestive tract has to work too hard to break down all that meal. God did not design our bodies for all of this. Milk is the next biggest cause of our health problems. There needs to be an equal amount of magnesium and calcium. Otherwise the body takes calcium from the bones and deposits it in the soft tissue. One theory about fibromyalgia is that this calcium is being deposited into the soft tissues of the body and calcifying. Many believe a virus is at the root cause. I contracted the shingles virus about one month after getting my silicone implants at age 29. This turned into post herpatic neuralgia 10 days after the ruptured disk in 1997.

I am in complete agreement with Reverend George Malkmus, minister and founder of Hallelujah Acres, the forerunner of Back to the Garden Health Ministries. He cured himself of colon cancer twenty-six years ago by going back to eating the way that God intended for us to eat as outlined in *Genesis 1: 29*. I'm not there yet, but I'm working on it. In reality, these truths are from a Biblical perspective. Sure, I've read it in the Bible before. Deep down in our hearts we all know that what I am talking about here is plain and simple truth. I should mention here that I am not trying to take any credit away from God, quite the contrary. He outlined it all in the Bible, and we know what we should eat and the way that we should live. As I stated before, I believe in divine, supernatural healing. However, God created our bodies to be able to heal themselves if we are putting the right things into them. We could receive a divine healing from God. However, continual abuse of our bodies by feeding them junk food will cause other problems to pop up from time to time. Now we have a choice. Unfortunately, people have been blinded to the truth, including Christians. The truth is that we are spirit, mind, and body, and we can't separate them. We are made up of all these things. It is true that we should follow after the Spirit, but that does not mean to neglect or abuse our physical bodies. Our bodies are a holy temple of the Living God, and we should take care of them. The text in the Bible that gets people off track, I think, is where it says "to be spiritually minded is life, to be carnally minded is death." Carnal has to do with the flesh. However, we must take care of our holy temples, our bodies. We should pray and ask the Holy Spirit what to eat. Being carnally minded is actually a mind set against Godly principles and values. I sometimes wonder if I would have ever gotten around to writing this book had the last few years of my life been any different. Don't get me wrong; sickness doesn't come from God. However, God (time after time) takes unfortunate circumstances and turns them around and uses them for His glory. God placed the desire in my heart several years ago to write this book and revealed to me in a dream that this is what He wanted me to do. Everything happens in God's own time. One thing is sure; my flesh has certainly not wanted to write this book, as you can well imagine. The spirit is strong, but the flesh is weak. All of us have high ideals, and everyone of us has a story to tell that could help other people. I just pray that my story will help some people. If I can leave this world knowing that, then I know that my Father in heaven will say with open arms, "Well done, My good and faithful servant."

Chapter Nine

Harvest Time

Proverbs 13: 22 "A good man leaveth an inheritance to his children's children: and the wealth of the sinner is laid up for the just."

Proverbs 28: 8: "He that by usury and unjust gain increaseth his substance, he shall gather it for him that will pity the poor."

Deuteronomy 6: 18: "And thou shalt do that which is right and good in the sight of the Lord: that it may be well with thee, and that thou mayest go in and possess the good land which the Lord sware unto thy fathers."

Job 27: 13-17: "This is the portion of a wicked man with God, and the heritage of oppressors, which they shall receive of the Almighty. If his children be multiplied it is for the sword: and his offspring shall not be satisfied with bread. Those that remain of him shall be buried in death: and his widows shall not weep. Though he heap up silver as the dust, and pre-pare raiment as the clay; He may prepare it, but the just shall put it on, and the innocent shall divide the silver."

Proverbs 8: 17-21: "I love them that love Me; and those that seek Me early shall find Me. Riches and honour are with Me; yea, durable riches and righteousness. My fruit is better than gold, yea, than fine gold; and My revenue than choice silver. I lead in the way of righ-teousness, in the midst of the paths of judgment: That I may cause those that love Me to inherit substance; and I will fill their treasures."

The first three Scriptures above refer to the truth that in the latter days God said that He would transfer the wealth of the wicked into the hands of righteous. Why will He do this? He will do it because He knows that the righteous will take the money and use it for the glory of God and for His Kingdom here on Earth to help usher people into heaven. When we leave this earthly plateau, the last dress or pair of pants that we will be wearing will not have any pockets. We can't take anything with us. Money is not the root of all evil; the love of money is the root of all evil. Money is just energy. The evil lies in the hearts of some of the people whose hands the money passes through. There is so much good that can be done for the Kingdom of God to bless people in so many ways, but things are way out of balance. God is in the process of balancing things in every way imaginable. The following Scriptures show us that God wants us to prosper:

Deuteronomy 8: 17-18: "And thou say in thine heart, my power and the might of mine hand hath gotten me this wealth. But thou shalt remember the Lord thy God: for it is He that giveth thee power to get wealth, that He may establish His covenant which He sware unto thy fathers, as it is this day."

Deuteronomy 8: 1-3: "All the commandments which I command thee this day shall ye observe to do, that ye may live, and multiply, and go in and possess the land which the Lord sware unto your fathers. And thou shalt remember all the way which the Lord thy God led thee these forty years in the wilderness, to humble thee, and to prove thee, to know what was in thine heart, whether thou wouldest keep His commandments, or no. And He humbled thee, and suf-

fered thee to hunger, and fed thee with manna, which thou knewest not, neither did thy fathers know; that He might make thee know that man doth not live by bread only, but by every word that proceedeth out of the mouth of the Lord doth man live."

To prosper means to acquire, procure, create, to harvest. The second verse of the third book of *John* tells us, *"Beloved, I wish above all things that thou mayest prosper and be in health, even as thy soul prospereth."* It is the amount of faith that you release when you act upon a spiritual revelation that determines your harvest in the natural world. The spiritual produces the natural so that you can prosper and be in health. However, you can't force another person to operate at your level of faith. The Holy Spirit dealing with each and every one of us is teaching each and every one of us. We are all learning the same lessons at different rates of speed. Some very strong willed people destroy themselves before getting their breakthrough due to pride and stubbornness. God is love, and He is always right there with us. You can feel His awesome presence in the stillness, in a crowd of people praising God, or even as a spectator in a somewhat hostile situation. As a spectator, we have a choice as to whether we want to turn our hearts and thoughts to God (thoughts of love and peace) or whether we want to tune in on the frequency of hate, revenge, judgment, etc. God said, "Be still and know that I am God." Many times, if we would just shut up, the bad feelings would just fade away involving a certain situation. The problem would work itself out on its own. Faith comes by hearing and hearing by the Word of God. It does not come by having heard it only once a month or even once a week. It comes by hearing and hearing and hearing on and on and on. The devil lies to people and tries to keep their minds focused on fears, doubts, problems, obstacles, sickness, lack of financial blessings, or all of these things. You must understand who your enemy is (Satan). God desires that you take a bold step of faith, believing that He will sustain you. If He didn't intend to remove problems or help you to overcome circumstances involving finances, He would never had said in *Deuteronomy 28: 12-13*:

> *"The Lord shall open unto thee His good treasure, the heaven to give the rain unto thy land in His season, and to bless all the word of thine hand: and thou shalt lend unto many nations and thou shalt not borrow. And the Lord shall make thee the head, and not the tail; and thou shalt be above only, and thou shalt not be beneath; if that thou hearken unto the commandments of the Lord*

thy God, which I command thee this day, to observe and do them."

Believers are beginning to wake up and learn not to settle for anything which tries to drain the Word of God of its power and effectiveness. You have tremendous potential inside of you right now. The secret is learning to use it to improve your life. However, you have the power of choice. *Deuteronomy 30: 19* says, *"I have set before you life and death, blessing and cursing: therefore choose life."* Fear of failure can keep you from your promised land, or you can drop the fear and move ahead and possess it. It is important to learn to harness the mind. The natural man's mind is uncontrolled. God gave us a brain through which His purposes for our lives could be fulfilled, but it is up to us to protect and nourish that brain. Our brains not only need the proper foods in order to function properly, they also need the proper spiritual food to ever reach our fullest potential.

Truth (spiritual values) must be accepted and life (carnal values) rejected. Truth subjects our minds to God's plan for our lives. It gives hope and defeats discouragement, which limits progress. Many believers, once they leave church on Sunday, never study God's Word and then quickly become carnal-minded again, thinking thoughts primarily dealing with the flesh. In church it is always easy to become spiritual-minded because the atmosphere has been created for you already. If you would like to become more spiritual-minded and far less carnal-minded, learn to create your own atmosphere wherever you are. Control your thoughts. You say you can't do that; I say you can. You may not always be able to control every thought that pops into your mind, and sometimes you wonder where some thoughts come from. However, you have the choice of entertaining those thoughts or lifting them up to God. You can learn to be not so easily influenced by how things look, and you also can learn to be not so easily moved by circumstances or feelings. These things are constantly changing, but God never changes. He is the same yesterday, today, and tomorrow. He knows all, sees all, and understands all. He is all you will ever need. Thousands of ideas pass through our minds daily. It requires only one good, sound, positive idea inspired from God and willingness to act upon it for it to become a reality. Ideas are like seeds and must be cultivated, watered, pruned, and developed, or they won't bare fruit. *Galatians 3: 29* says, *"And if ye be Christ's, then are ye Abraham's seed, and heirs according to the promise."*

According to *Proverbs 13: 22*, *"the wealth of the sinner is laid up for the just"* (those who trust God). A person who has made sinning a daily part of his life does not understand how to operate in spiritual laws. Wealth is what we have inside of us. *Hebrews 11: 1* says that *"faith is the substance of things hoped for, the evidence of things not seen."* Wisdom, information, and the ability to see things with our spirit is what will produce abundance in our lives. *Proverbs 3:16* promises that *"Length of days is in her right hand; and in her left hand riches and honour,"* and *Matthew* assures us that *"where your treasure is, there will your heart be also."* Principles of prayer, faith, and hard work still aren't enough. You must have a vision, a burning desire. *Proverbs 29: 18a* says, *"Where there is no vision, the people perish."* However, for our vision to be fulfilled, God must always be first. We should obey what *Matthew 6: 33* tells us: *"But seek ye first the Kingdom of God, and His righteousness; and all these things shall be added unto you."* When a person trusts in riches instead of God, that person becomes greedy, investments turn sour, and riches vanish.

God can't bless you beyond your level of expectancy, and expecting comes after a seed is sown, which is an act of faith. This is what God sees and what God honors. *Isaiah 1: 19* says, *"If ye be willing and obedient, ye shall eat the good of the land."* God's promises are founded on willingness and obedience, not on wishful thinking. Every action has a reaction. You cause things to happen by your actions of faith. *Luke 6: 38* tells us to *"Give, and it shall be given unto you; good measure, pressed down, and shaken together, and running over, shall men give into your bosom. For with the same measure that ye mete withal it shall be measured to you again."* I know some of you are thinking that all you really want is just enough to get by. I can assure you that if that is all you ever really want and you express that all the time, then that is exactly what you will get. *James 4: 2* says *"ye have not, because ye ask not."* Before you can ever change any of your present circumstances, you must understand, accept, and believe what God said. He does want you, yes, even little old you, to prosper. However, you need to make your praying and your saying the same. Don't say one thing and in prayer try to believe God for something else. The doubt cancels out the faith. The Bible is full of Scriptures that reveal God's promises:

Romans 8: 32: "He that spared not His own Son, but deliv-
ered Him up for us all, how shall He not with Him
also freely give us all things?"
Psalms 37: 4: "Delight thyself also in the Lord; and He shall
give thee the desires of thine heart."

Psalms 34: 10: "The young lions do lack, and suffer hunger: but they that seek the Lord shall not want any good thing."

Psalms 84: 11: "For the Lord God is a sun and shield: the Lord will give grace and glory: no good thing will He withhold from them that walk uprightly."

2 Chronicles 26: 5: "And he [King Uzziah] sought God in the days of Zechariah, who had understanding in the visions of God: and as long as he sought the Lord, God made him to prosper."

As I mentioned in a previous chapter, tithing is very important. It can't be stressed enough, though many people feel pressured when preachers begin to talk about tithing. *First Corinthians 16: 2* commands, *"Upon the first day of the week let every one of you lay by him in store, as God hath prospered him, that there be no gatherings when I come."* The tithe already belongs to God; that is His money. Actually, it all belongs to Him. He gives it all to us. The least we can do is to give back to Him ten percent for His Kingdom. God has given us power to get wealth. In the Hebrew language, that means to get, make, create, design, invent, bring forth, procure, bring into being, or cause to happen. The abundant blessings of God come through offerings (money, service, time) over and above the tithes which are already His. God created us, and He is the One Who gives us the intelligence to do these things. He must be given credit for everything. He is a very jealous God, and one way or the other, He knows how to get our attention; He will be acknowledged. You can put Him on a shelf for a little while, but you will regret it.

God already knows all the problems that we have gone through, that we are going through now, or that we will face in the future. He does not want us to come to Him crying over the problem. His Word says in *Mark 11: 23, "For verily I say unto you, That whosoever shall say unto this mountain, Be thou removed, and be thou cast into the sea; and shall not doubt in his heart, but shall believe that those things which he saith shall come to pass; he shall have whatsoever he saith."* After you read, contemplate, pray, and digest God's promises, you must go out and claim your possessions. You must walk out in faith, in total expectancy of your good to come forth. You must have corresponding actions of faith, and this requires work. Laziness will never get God's blessings or prosperity. Believers are learning how to change and to rule their environment. *James 1: 6-8* states, *"But let him ask in faith, nothing wavering. For he that wavereth is like a wave of the sea driven with wind and tossed. For let not that man think that he shall receive any thing of the Lord. A double minded man is unstable in all his ways."* As a born-again Christian, you are an heir of Abraham, Isaac, Jacob, and the Abrahamic covenant is yours. It is your inheritance, and there is nothing wrong with claiming what belongs to you. Success is your birthright, and you don't need to apologize for it. When God's Word becomes your foundation and your sword, your house will not fall. Your Christian walk will not fail. Jesus promises in *Matthew 16: 19* that He will give us *"the keys of the Kingdom of heaven."* The following Scriptures tell what God has in store for the Christian:

2 Chronicles 20:20: "Believe in the Lord your God, so shall ye be established; believe His prophets, so shall ye prosper.

Job 36: 11: "If they obey and serve Him, they shall spend their days in prosperity, and their in pleasures."

2 Peter 1: 3: "According as His divine power hath given unto us all things that pertain unto life and godliness, through the knowledge of Him that hath called us to glory and virtue."

Luke 9: 56: "For the Son of man is not come to destroy men's lives, but to save them."

However, Jesus warned in *Luke 9: 62*, *"No man, having put his hand to the plough, and looking back, is fit for the Kingdom of God."*

So many people are missing out on so much joy that they could be experiencing today by continually bringing up past heartaches and pain, laying hurt feelings out on a table, and analyzing moves and actions on other people's parts and their own relating to past negative events. They are playing right into Satan's hands, allowing him to zap the joy from the present moment. There is no guarantee of tomorrow; all you have is today, so how can we keep this from happening? If it is your spouse continually bringing up the past, you need to be a good listener and a good friend and gently help your spouse to realize what is happening. As long as a person continually brings up things that other people have done to him/her in the past, then that person has not learned how to forgive. What these people need to understand is that they are not hurting other people by not forgiving them. They are only hurting themselves. Those other people have more than likely gone on down the road and long forgotten about the incident. For their sakes and for Christ's sake, we need to forgive. Hopefully, as people learn to draw closer to God and spend more time with Him, they will eventually learn this hard lesson. A person can learn to mentally forgive someone even if he can't bring himself to forgive face to face. I believe that unforgiveness can cause many health problems. If we are walking around with all this bitterness inside, then we are putting out bad vibrations. Other people pick up on these, and we are causing ourselves even more grief and heartache. Negativism breeds negativism. It is in God that we live and move and have our being, and God is love. Oh, for grace to trust Him more. Good follows good; bad follows bad. God is in control of everything. We all have the same lessons to learn. As long as we continue to do the same things, then we will get the same results. There is a purpose for every life here on Earth, and God created us for His pleasure, not for our own. We are called to have faith like that of a little child. We are His children, and He loves each and every one of us. As we learn to understand the concept that we are His children and just how much He loves us, we begin to trust Him more and more to meet every need. He wants so much to shower blessing upon blessing on His children, but outright disobedience to God hurts Him. Disobedience blocks the majority of the blessings. If we know something is wrong and we do it anyway, then we are disobeying God. We are obeying God if we are listening to His still, small voice and doing what He says to do. You can hear this voice if you get still before the Lord long enough.

God must be first and foremost in our lives before He is willing to shower us with all His blessings. If God is not first in a person's life, then that person is still in bondage to unforgiveness of other people and himself. If they would choose forgiveness for themselves, then it would be easier to forgive others. To be able to forgive one's self, one must embrace the full love of God by repenting and inviting Jesus into his heart.

There is absolutely no reason to walk around in fear or in a panic continually expecting bad things to happen. If you are praying for good things but speaking about bad things, then where is the faith? The negative things are canceling out the faith and trust that God will bring about the good. God owns everything. The supply is endless; there is no shortage of anything. There is plenty of love, kindness, gentleness, patience, peace, money, and good health, but here's the catch. We must be sowing them ourselves in order to get them back from others. God can only do for us that which He can do through us. It is up to each human being to line up one' s heart and spirit with the Living Word of God and to get into a position where one feels worthy of God's blessings. Only by spending time at the cross and believing that we have been redeemed from the curse because Jesus died for us, can we begin to fully expect God's blessings. However, faith without works is dead. Action is required as well as faith in order to move forward, fully expecting God's blessings. God is able to do exceedingly and abundantly above all we could ever hope for or ask for. *Luke 12: 31* tells us to *"seek ye the Kingdom of God; and all these things shall be added unto you."* The ten great commandments are exactly what they say they are. They are commandments. They are not merely suggestions or multiple choices. *Matthew 22: 37-40* repeats God's commandments. *"Thou shalt love the Lord thy God with all thy heart, and with all thy soul, and with all thy mind. This is the first and great commandment. And the second is like unto it, Thou shalt love thy neighbour as thyself. On these two commandments hang all the law and prophets."* We can further demonstrate our faith in God by remembering the promise in Jeremiah 33: 3: *"Call unto Me, and I will answer thee, and shew thee great and mighty things, which thou knowest not."* However, *Hosea 4: 6* warns, *"My people are destroyed for lack of knowledge: because thou hast rejected knowledge, I will also reject thee..."*

The liberty and freedom from bondage and the grace to trust in God and His perfect plan for all mankind happens as a person chooses the path of righteousness, sometimes after a long, inner struggle. God freely gives this choice to each individual, but the inner man or woman must be changed before any outward changes will be manifest. *Psalms 1: 1-3* tells us who God will bless:

> *"Blessed is the man that walketh not in the counsel of the ungodly, nor standeth in the way of sinners, nor sitteth in the seat of the scornful. But his delight is in the law of the Lord; and in His law doth he meditate day and night. And he shall be like a tree planted by the rivers of water, that bringeth forth his fruit in his season; his leaf also shall not wither; and whatsoever he doeth shall prosper."*

Good stewardship is a primary key to obtaining wealth. The quality of that stewardship determines your level. We must learn to become good stewards of that which God has given us in order for Him to give us more. Here we are speaking primarily of material or financial blessings. If we don't take care of what He has already given us, how can we expect Him to give us any more? This has to do with developing an attitude of gratitude. There is much power in being grateful. God expects us to use the gifts that He has bestowed on us. He makes this very clear in the twenty-fifth chapter of *Matthew*. Learning to develop one talent and use it wisely and especially for God's glory will serve to propel you to even greater talents. To whom much is given, much shall be expected. God does not give us all these talents just to benefit ourselves. He gives them to us to use for His glory, not ours. However, we do benefit tremendously as a result of this obedience to Him.

Philippians commands us to *"Rejoice in the Lord alway: and again I say, Rejoice."* You can learn to rejoice even during a down time. It isn't easy to come to this place, but you can. The more you learn to trust God, the easier it becomes. It is in the valleys of life that we learn to draw nearer to God and learn to depend on Him. Without the valleys, how could we ever grow in faith? I have learned, no matter what, that I must continue to praise God. Satan wants to destroy us with fears and doubts concerning anything and everything that he can, including trying to destroy our loved ones. I have made up my mind that he is not winning in my case. I have discovered one thing that Satan is extremely disturbed over is the believer's faith in his authority through God. This authority should never be taken lightly. It is the exercising of this authority that will help to put you over into the blessing realm of life for you and your loved ones. The battles of life are first won in the spiritual realm before they are made manifest in the physical realm. If you learn nothing from this book but that one truth, then I have done a magnificent work for the Kingdom of God. Glory to God!!

One of the worst years of my life was 1998. Not only did I begin suffering from physical pain in October, 1997, when I had the ruptured disk, but the mental anguish in dealing with problems associated with both my sons was almost more than I could bear, or so it seemed at the time. I'm sure you know what I mean; we all go through trials. Many are the afflictions of the righteous, but the Lord delivers the righteous out of all them. In addition to all the problems related to my sons and my health, we had seven deaths in our family from July, 1996 to October, 1997. First, my stepfather of fourteen years died. He was so good to my mother; he treated her wonderfully, and we all loved him dearly. Three months later, my brother-in-law, a part of our family for over forty years, died of lung cancer. It was like losing a brother to me. Then my uncle in Mobile died. Shortly after that, his wife, Aunt Clara, died, and then two cousins in New Orleans died. After that, my oldest sister in New Orleans passed away. Just before she died, I thought my heart would break in two when, after arriving in New Orleans with two of my sisters and a brother-in-law, I walked into that intensive care unit and first looked at Jeanette. She was nothing but skin stretched over bones. She had starved herself to death over a twenty-year period. She had never recovered from her husband of fourteen years leaving her for another woman. Even with the apparent unforgiveness involved here, I still believe that she had accepted Jesus before she left this world. I had written to her and sent her paintings of the Lord and poems I had written about the Lord. Despite how it may have appeared to other people, I feel at peace in my heart that she had a personal relationship with our Lord and Savior, Jesus Christ.

In June of 1998 I received a phone call from the girl who had lived with my oldest son's father for over twenty years. She was suggesting that I put my son, Paris in a mental hospital. It seems that there was quite a bit of confusion, to say the least, concerning the relationship between Paris and his father. For you to understand this situation fully, I must explain further. His father left me for a gay man, an English professor in Tallahassee, Florida, when Paris was four years old. Never dreaming that anything would happen to Paris, I allowed him to visit for a weekend with his father. I later learned not long after that weekend that the man had molested my son. As you can imagine, I had all kinds of mixed emotions. My first thought was to go down there and confront him, ruin his career, or have him arrested, or whatever I could do. I talked with his father over the phone about the matter, and he denied outright that the incident could have ever taken place. I believed it had. At twenty-three years of age, at least back then, one didn't think about all the emotional problems a child could suffer from being molested. Only in the last few years have all these facts come to light with all the talk shows on television, etc. At any rate, I decided at that time that I would never question my son about it again. I would just try to forgive and forget that it had ever happened, hoping he would never remember. This was the wrong way to handle the situation. Though I did not allow my son to go anywhere near that man again, I never talked in a negative way about his father to him until he was twelve years old and the subject of gay people came up. Then I felt like he was old enough to accept what had happened. As I told him what had happened, big old crocodile tears ran down his cheeks. He said, "Mom, I thought that was just a bad dream all these years." I was struggling to make ends meet and of course couldn't afford to get him any kind of therapy. I just tried to talk to him about the need to forgive and to put it behind us. His father had left the gay man and developed a lifelong relationship with a woman. It's strange sometimes how things work out. In 1996 Paris (age 31) lived within three miles of his father and Sharon. Wayne had never paid any child support except one check for sixty dollars, and he had managed to stay out of the state all those years until long after Paris was entitled to child support. Then Wayne and Sharon came home to buy property and settle down. Of course there were problems between Paris and his father. His father would never admit that the molestation ever could have occurred. Wayne also had tremendous emotional problems because he had been sexually abused as a teenager by a close relative himself. It had been heavily rumored that Wayne and Sharon were dealing drugs quite heavily, even though she managed to maintain a public job, usually in an executive position such as a hospital administrator. When she called me in June of 1998 concerning Paris, I had prayed with her and Wayne on the phone. I knew then that this situation was serious. Paris was threatening to commit suicide, and Sharon suggested that I put him in the Chattahoochee State Mental Hospital. He had been labeled with a bipolar disorder. I called him that night, and he could hardly talk. I prayed and prayed and finally felt some peace that God had the situation in His hands. The next morning my niece, Darlene, and I went to visit Paris. When we got close by, I called Paris on the phone. When he answered, I just broke down crying and praising God that he was all right. I would not make the decision for Paris to go into a state hospital. I told him he would have to make that decision, and he decided that he should. The way he described it to me was that he was seeing things melt before his very eyes. The chemicals in his brain were unbalanced. My niece, Darlene, and I took him to Life Management in Panama City, Florida. Darlene has a Master's Degree in psychology, and she thought that this would be the best way to go about the whole ordeal of trying to get him some help. He stayed there a few days and then decided he wanted to go home after they got him stabilized. He still had some horrific times after that until the medication was adjusted and stabilized more. During all this time I was praying fervently about five times a day and crying and pleading with the Lord, but primarily I was taking authority over the devil and letting him know in no uncertain terms that he could not have my son, that my son was a child of God, and that God had plans for his life. I praise God that Paris decided at that time to stay away from Wayne and Sharon. Six months later Sharon shot and killed Wayne on Thanksgiving night, 1998. This was devastating to Paris because he wanted so badly to have a loving relationship with his father.

Paris had been dealing with the fact that his pancreas had totally shut down and that he had been diabetic for over two years. He had become quite withdrawn; however, praise God that he is an overcomer. He is a survivor by the grace of God. Paris started working with fiber optics, had a good job, earning good money, and I was so proud of him. He bought a brand new Harley Davidson motorcycle and paid cash for it, so he was doing quite well on the surface.

As I finish this final re-write of the book I want to share some wonderful things that have been going on with Paris – actually some wonderful and some not so wonderful. I keep remembering the question: "Is the glass half empty of hall full?" I have always chosen to see it (at least most of the time) as being half full. Paris spent four months in a Christian Missions Rehab Program for drugs and alcohol in Enterprise, Alabama, about 35 miles from Dothan. He had finally reached his bottom and had nowhere to turn but to the Lord. It is so amazing what the Lord has done in his life and what He continues to do. This program is run by Almighty God Himself. There is no amount of money that could ever buy this type of treatment, and by the grace of God, there is no charge. It is a twelve step Christian program. The students are there strictly because the Holy Spirit is keeping them there. A few drop out as time goes along. Praise God Paris was determined to stay in the program, although he was tempted and Satan tried hard to kick him out of the program; but he has a prayer warrior for a Mother. They listened to a preacher for three hours every day. They had devotion every morning and every night. They had one on one counseling once a week or however much they may have needed it. There were always counselors (some of which have been through the program previously) on hand to pray with them, lead them, and guide them, and just be there for them, no matter what they were going through. They worked at a retail outlet that the ministry owns and operates. They were free to go home on weekends, but many chose not to leave. They had very strict rules and guidelines to go by. They had a support group meeting on Tuesday nights. People who have been through the program years before come to the group meetings because of the love of Jesus in their hearts and the compassion for the new people in the program. Family members come and they usually always have a speaker who tells their story. The speakers always touch the deepest parts of people's hearts, as they sit there sometimes and listen and weep. Then they have open discussion, where anyone can talk. Over the course of the months when I went to the meetings I was blessed beyond measure, and I sat there and listened to them share many of their difficulties from the bottom of their heart and yet turn around and witness for the Lord, giving Him the glory for what He is doing in their lives. It is truly awesome.

Just before Paris entered the program he started going to NA Meetings, and to Church. He loves the people he is meeting and the Lord continues to use him to witness to many people, some who have mentioned the idea of suicide. In 2006 Paris wrecked his motorcycle, a $30,000 Harley Davidson. Once again the blood of Jesus was covering him. He totaled the bike and only, by the grace of God, had a compound fracture in his left leg. He has a steel rod from the knee down. God has heard my fervent prayers crying out and pleading the blood of Jesus over him and taking authority over the devil. Satan will not have my son. God has a mighty plan for his life. Paris is just now beginning to realize this. He that has begun a good work will complete it. God is filling him up to overflowing with His perfect love. Paris is a living, walking, breathing miracle from God, and is blessed beyond measure.

My younger son, Brent, who lives in Hawaii is a miracle, as well. However, I am not at liberty to share his story at this time. His story is so awesome that it would not be fair to him to diminish the amazing power of Almighty God. I am certain that God will get the glory in His perfect diving timing. He has a special anointing upon his life and is very gifted with his music through the guitar, and piano.

What has all this to do with harvest time? As far as I'm concerned, it has everything to do with it. Harvest time is a time when all things are returned to God. Consider these verses of Scripture:

Isaiah 49: 25: "But thus saith the Lord, even the captives of the mighty shall be taken away, and the prey of the terrible shall be delivered: for I will contend with him that contendeth with thee, and I will save thy children."

Isaiah 54: 13: "And all thy children shall be taught of the Lord; and great shall be the peace of thy children."

Jeremiah 1: 5: "Before I formed thee in the belly I knew thee; and before thou camest forth out of the womb I sanctified thee, and I ordained thee a prophet unto the nations."

Some other Scriptures that I highly recommend for daily confessions over your children, in which I have substituted the words my children to show you how to personalize God's promises, are as follows:

Psalms 37: 23: "The steps of my children are ordered by the Lord; and He delighteth in his way."

Luke 2: 52: "And my children increased in wisdom and stature, and in favour with God and man."

Isaiah 10: 27: *"And it shall come to pass in that day, that my children's burdens shall be taken away from off their shoulders, and his yoke from off their necks, and the yoke shall be destroyed because of the anointing."*

Colossians 2: 2: *"My children's hearts might be comforted, being knit together in love, and unto all riches of the full assurance of understanding, to the acknowledgement of the mystery of God, and of the Father, and of Christ."*

John 10: 4: *"My children follow Him (the Lord): for they know His voice."*

Romans 5: 17: *"My children receive abundance of grace and of the gift of righteousness shall reign in life by one, Jesus Christ."*

2 Corinthians 2: 11: *"Now thanks be unto God, which always causeth my children to triumph in Christ..."*

Psalms 37: 11: *"My children shall delight themselves in the abundance of peace."*

In affirming these promises often, I name my sons specifically. I know that God's words do not return unto Him void but accomplish that which they are sent forth to accomplish! We can rest in the assurance of these Scriptures:

Genesis 17: 7-8: "And I will establish my covenant between Me and thee and thy seed after thee in their genera-tions for an everlasting covenant, to be a God unto thee, and to thy seed after thee. And I will give unto thee, and to thy seed after thee, the land wherein thou art a stranger, all the land of Canaan, for an ever-lasting possession; and I will be their God."

Galatians 3: 29: "And if ye be Christ's, then are ye Abraham's seed, and heirs according to the promise."

I also believe that learning to become healthy has a lot to do with the harvest. We want to gather in all the informa-tion that we can and bring in all the healthy bodies that we can. Even though we should not be overly consumed with our bodies, we should take care of them. They are a temple of the Holy Spirit. If we are suffering from physical prob-lems that seem to linger on and on, then perhaps we need to identify what toxic substance could possibly be causing our health problems, learn how to eliminate them, and get on with our lives. This is where I am now. I have not accepted what ninety-five percent of the literature that I have read about fibromyalgia, myofascial pain syndrome, chronic pain syndrome, and osteoporosis say about all of these things. I believe that God is giving me the wisdom that I need to overcome all my health challenges.

After several years of researching all of the many varied symptoms concerning my health challenges, at the beginning of 2001 I discovered for certain that most of my health issues stemmed from Silicone poison. I had my implants for over 30 years. About 6 months prior to this I had come across a website on the internet and all the symptoms these people with Silicone problems were describing were exactly what I had been experiencing for a long, long time. However, after having an ultrasound, a Silicone antibodies test, and an MRI with a Breast Coil, I was told that my implants were fine, not ruptured, everything was OK. I kept digging and talking to the women in the International Silicone Support Group and decided that the implants had to come out for the following reasons:

1. In the fall of 1996 I had a chest x-ray and it looked very suspicious to me. The doctor agreed and sent me to another doctor. I had no insurance at the time. The second doctor told me that his wife had silicone implants and he suggested I leave them alone. So I put it out of my mind. I was not shown the actual report

from the Radiologist specifically indicating that one was probably ruptured. I saw this report years later.

2. Silicone Implants contain over 40 known neuro-toxins – just to name a few – Lacquer Thinner, Epoxy Hardener, Epoxy Resin, Printing Ink, Freon, Formaldehyde, and Rubber. Silicone was meant to be Transmission Fluid back in the 50s when it first came out.

3. It came out in the original FDA trials of the Class Action Silicone Law Suit when the pharmaceutical sales people would take the implants to the doctors they would wipe them off, as they had been instructed to do, because many doctors complained that they were leaking (very tiny minute leaks). Over the course of having them 30 years much Silicone had escaped and was running rampant throughout my entire body. Two months after being implanted my immune system was compromised.

4. It became quite clear to me that in the Spring of 1996 when I had the collapsing sensation on my right side, which I contributed to Pneumonia at the time, that my right implant had indeed ruptured. I now know in my spirit, despite what all the so-called medical tests

were showing, that Silicone was wrecking havoc on my body.

5. It became quite clear to me that any time you put a foreign object into the body, that by God's own design the body will automatically begin to attack it. The immune system is very intelligent and knows what to do. When the immune system is having to work continuously to try to destroy something that isn't supposed to be there then you have auto-immune problems. You have an overactive immune system. This is just as bad as having an underactive immune system.

6. Over a period of eight years I was diagnosed with:
    a. Osteoporosis
    b. Scoliosis
    c. Osteoarthritis
    d. Fibromyalgia
    e. Myofascial Pain Syndrome
    f. Angina
    g. Candida (overgrowth of bad bacteria in GI tract)
    h. Hypothyroidism
    i. Shingles (contracted them one month after getting implants)

j. Post Herpetic Neuralgia

k. Chronic Fatigue Immune Deficiency Syndrome

l. Connective Tissue Disorder (Silicone Adjuvant Disease)

m. Degenerative Bone Disease

n. Cataracts

o. Chemical Sensitivity

p. Muscular Degeneration

q. Pneumonia (twice)

r. Imbalanced Hormones

s. Hepatitis B

t. Gout

u. Neuropathy

v. Allergies

w. Macular Degeneration

x. Irritable Bowel Syndrome

The bottom line and root core cause of all the numerous overlapping symptoms relating to all these diagnoses is SILICONE. There are no ifs, ands, or buts about it. I am here to tell you that everything you have heard about Silicone is TRUE. Yet women still to this day prefer the solid silicone to the saline. On that subject, let it be known that Saline itself may be harmless to the human body. However, saline implants are encapsulated in a Silicone Elastomer Shell. There is also a Saline Class Action Law Suit. Many women are actually having a fungus growing inside the implant. Many women have this happening right now inside their bodies and they don't even know it. Please understand I don't mean to project fear but I am concerned for people. It shows up on some MRIs.

There is so much money and power behind this Silicone issue. It came out in one of the Canadian magazines a few years ago that this is how deep the politics go: Dow Chemical is owned and operated by a big conglomerate called RANK. On their board of directors sits one of the Royal brothers from England. There is a lot of money and a lot of power relating to the silicone issues.

It breaks my heart to see women getting implants right and left. Girls eighteen and even younger today are getting implants to boost their self esteem. It doesn't work. Unfortunately they will pay the price sooner or later. How sad it is.

At any rate, two years later, after my ex-plant, I was still having challenges. However, the light at the end of the tunnel no longer looked like a freight train coming at me, Praise God. They tell me it takes three to five years to totally

DETOX the human body. By the grace of Almighty God I have managed to stay away from pharmaceutical drugs. I have studied Nutrition to the point where I feel like I should have a degree in it, but unfortunately I don't.

Recently I have studied extensively about amino acids and how you can use them to heal the body. You can find a wealth of helpful information in the book *Heal With Amino Acids* written by two PHDs. I have also re-discovered and read a book titled *The Power of Your Subconscious Mind*, which I had read twenty years ago. It is based on the Bible and it is truly an awesome book, in my opinion.

I still have some challenges like everyone has, but God has brought me a mighty long way. When I first came back to Barrows Furniture to work in December of 2004 I thought I was going to die. I had to push through the pain for three months walking up and down stairs and being on my feet a good portion of the day. But healed people go to work and the price for my healing and yours was paid over 2000 years ago. By His stripes I was healed. Therefore, if I was healed, then I am healed. I am still working.

There have been times when I begged God to take my life, the pain would be so unbearable. There have been times when I literally could not hold up a song book in church because of the sudden onset of overwhelming fatigue. There have been over 85 symptoms to deal with. But, through it all, God has always been right here with me, leading me and guiding me, and I have learned to trust in Him to such a degree that just amazes even myself. (Amazing Grace – How Sweet The Sound). He does indeed give us grace to go through anything and everything. No problem is too big for our God. He is far bigger than any problem Satan could ever or will ever throw at us. God is in control. I trust in Him with all my heart and I lean not unto my own understanding. I acknowledge Him in all my ways, and He directs my paths, and all is well with my soul. By His stripes we are healed. We must cling to the Word of God and God's promises. They are real. They are TRUTH and His truth far supersedes any and all so-called facts here in this earthly realm. His promises will come to pass if you BELIEVE they will. But you must develop a persistent and tenacious spirit. Never give up. Understand Satan can not do any more to you than you allow him to. He can only slow us down and attempt to wear us out. That is all the power he has. His days are numbered and he knows it.

God is taking all the things that Satan has tried to use to destroy me and turning them completely around for His glory. What I want you to know is that God will turn your situation around, also. You are special. You are valuable. You have a story. Why not tell it? There are people who need to hear your story to know they are not alone.

In the meantime, I will not allow my challenges to hold me back from sharing what I have learned thus far. Fasting can be one way to help bring about a healthier body.

Many Scriptures throughout the Bible give reference to the benefits of fasting. To gain some new insight on fasting, I recommend that one study the following Scriptures:

3 John 2	*Deuteronomy 11: 7-15, 21*	*Luke 9: 11*
Matthew 9: 9-15	*2 Corinthians 7: 5*	*Galatians 5: 13-26*
Mark 2: 16-20	*Nehemiah 9: 1, 20-24*	*2 Corinthians 6*
Isaiah 58	*Matthew 4: 1-4*	*Psalms 35: 13*
Deuteronomy 8: 3	*James 5: 10-20*	*Matthew 6: 6-18*
Romans 16: 16-20	*Genesis 6: 3*	*John 15*
Matthew 7	*Zechariah 8: 19*	

Fasting is routine for the animal kingdom. It has been a commonplace experience since man's existence. Fasting is also a rite in all religions; the Bible alone has seventy-four references to it. To fast is not to starve; it is nature's cure that God has given us. Under proper conditions, it is absolutely safe. Fasting can be one way to help bring about a healthier body. Following are some of the benefits that we can derive from fasting:

- Easier than any diet; the quickest way to lose weight
- Adaptable to a busy life; gives the body a physiological rest
- Used successfully in the treatment of many physical illnesses
- Lowers and normalizes cholesterol and blood pressure levels
- A calming experience that often relieves tension and insomnia
- Improves dietary habits and increases eating pleasure
- Frequently induces feelings of euphoria, a natural high
- A rejuvenator that slows the aging process
- An energizer, not a debilitator; aids the elimination process
- Can eliminate or modify smoking, drug, and drinking addictions
- A regulator that educates the body to consume food only as needed
- Saves time spent marketing, preparing food, and eating
- Rids the body of toxins, giving it an "internal shower" and cleansing
- Does not deprive the body of essential nutrients
- Used effectively in schizophrenia treatment and other mental illnesses

- Can be tolerated up to four weeks under proper supervision
- Does not accumulate appetite; hunger pangs disappear in one or two days

If you have never fasted before, I certainly would not suggest a total, complete fast to begin with. You might start with leaving off one meal a day. I will be completely honest with you. My experience with fasting has been quite minimal through the years. I have fasted for as long as three days, but I always drank juice throughout the day. This is okay. It is still quite beneficial to the body. A few years ago, my chiropractor suggested that I go on a fast for three days with water only, no vitamins. I had never done that before. For two days I did fine. I had just bought my computer, so I kept myself busy. Food didn't cross my mind much at all. The third day I woke up extremely weak, so I began drinking some natural organic juice that I bought at the health food store. I want to discipline myself to fast one day a week and three days a month. I believe this will be very beneficial. Most precious of all is that fasting draws us more fully into the presence of God.

I believe we are living in a time of renewal, restoration, and revival, Praise God!! *John 4: 35* says, *"Lift up your eyes,*

and look on the fields; for they are white already to harvest."
Israel was gathered together as a nation in 1948. This means
that now is the time of Jubilee – a party, a celebration. Now
God's timing is not the same as ours. This is what the Bible
says about the Year of Jubilee:

Leviticus 25: 8-13: "And thou shalt number seven sabbaths
of years unto thee, seven times seven years; and the
space of the seven sabbaths of years shall be unto
thee forty and nine years. Then shalt thou cause the
trumpet of the jubile to sound on the tenth day of the
seventh month, in the day of atonement shall ye make
the trumpet sound throughout all your land. And
ye shall hallow the fiftieth year, and proclaim lib-
erty throughout all the land unto all the inhabitants
thereof: it shall be a jubile unto you; and ye shall
return every man unto his possession, and ye shall
return every man unto his family. A jubile shall that
fiftieth year be unto you: ye shall not sow, neither
reap that which groweth of itself in it, nor gather the
grapes in it of thy vine undressed. For it is the jubile;
it shall be holy unto you: ye shall eat the increase
thereof out of the field. In the year of this jubile ye
shall return every man unto his possession."

Everything returns unto God in the Year of Jubilee. I have never seen so many people so hungry for God in my entire life as there are today. Evangelists all over the world are bringing in the harvest of souls that have been thirsting and hungering for God. We are getting wind of this happening on secular television since 9-11. In order to find out what wonderful things are going on around the world for the glory of God and for His Kingdom here on Earth and in the world hereafter, get involved with a church and turn to Christian television. These are the people who have the deepest compassion for your complete well-being, not only while you are here in this world, but for eternal life.

Whatever the question is, Jesus is the answer!! He alone can fill the void in the human heart. It is time to quit searching for other things to fill this void; nothing or no one else can. God created us that way. Jesus said, *"I am the way, the truth, and the life. No man cometh unto the Father except by Me."* Jesus is God; Jesus was God made manifest in the flesh. God can manifest Himself as anything He wants to at anytime. He manifested Himself as a burning bush, didn't He? Jesus loves you with all His heart. It is up to you to embrace that love, to choose to believe that He loves you. The only way you will ever be totally free is to accept the love of Jesus, to repent of your sins, and to declare that He is your Lord and

Savior. God can do for you *only* what He can do *through* you.

There are many souls yet to be won for the Kingdom of God. We must take this assignment from the Lord seriously. We must take care of our Holy temples so that we are able to do the work God has called us to do. To whom much is given, much shall be required.

Has God done a lot for you? I believe the height of selfishness is to keep Jesus a secret. He said, if we are not ashamed of Him, then He will not be ashamed of us *(Matthew 9: 37)*. *The harvest truly is plenteous, but the labourers are few; Pray ye therefore the Lord of the harvest, that He will send forth labourers into His harvest (Matthew 9: 37, 38).*

Chapter Ten

You Are More Than a Conqueror

Praise is God's home address. God's Word says that He resides in the praises of His people. God is free to manifest Himself to you in what He is when you praise Him. Praise is our prime weapon against Satan. Let's reclaim it! Listed below are some of the names of God and what they mean:

Jehovah Jireh – My source, my sufficiency; my provider

Jehovah Rohpe – My health; my healing; my physician

Jehovah Nissi – My flag; my banner; my victory

Jehovah Mkaddesh – My light; my holiness; my sanctity

Jehovah Shalom – My peace; my comfort; my security

Jehovah Rohi – My guide; my shepherd; my protector

Jehovah Tsidkenu – My life; my redemption; my righteousness

Jehovah Shammah – My friend; my faithfulness; omnipresent

Let's begin to exalt our Heavenly Father more often. Let's begin to call Him by His names. Let's begin to claim the blessings that God wants us to have. Let's give Him the glory, and He will give us the victory over every situation we could ever encounter. The Bible tells us to *"Seek ye first the Kingdom of God, and all things will be added unto you."* Blessings flow to those who are running in God's destiny, in other words to those who have fallen totally in love with Jesus and have chosen to put Him first and foremost in their lives, no matter what. Everything happens in God's own timing. To everything there is a season. However, you must learn to be sensitive to the Holy Spirit to be able to make the right choices. God is always gently nudging us, but He will never force Himself on us. God sends precisely the right people at precisely the right time into your life to help you to stretch your faith and to reach up for a little bit higher level from which to view things. If we are learning to open ourselves up as willing vessels of His love, then we can climb higher and higher, and there is nothing that shall be impossible with God. It is not our own strength at work, but it is

God working in us and through us. It is in God that we live and move and have our being. *Psalms 103: 20-22* reminds us to *"Bless the Lord, ye His angels, that excel in strength, that do His commandments, hearkening unto the voice of His Word. Bless the Lord, all ye His hosts; ye ministers of His, that do His pleasure. Bless the Lord, all His works in all places of His dominion: bless the Lord, O my soul."* Matthew *18: 3-4* tells us how to enter God's Kingdom: *"Except ye be converted, and become as little children, ye shall not enter into the Kingdom of heaven. Whosoever therefore shall humble himself as this little child, the same is greatest in the Kingdom of heaven."*

It requires a child-like faith to learn how to trust God and to walk in His ways. As adults, it is sometimes hard for us to do because we tend to want to take control. Many times we don't get what we are praying for because God has something much better in store for us. Listed below are just some of the many roadblocks that Satan tries to use against us to keep us from stretching our faith to reach higher goals. Do you recognize any of these?

1. Color of skin (being in a minority)
2. Lack of education
3. Thinking yourself too old or too young

4. The way someone looks

5. Physical handicaps

6. Abuses that linger in the mind

7. No one listening

8. Resenting favorite children of parents

9. Being taken advantage of financially

10. Not being born into a Christian family

11. Didn't go to Bible school

12. No supernatural call

13. Bad marriage

14. Bad habits

15. Low self-esteem

Destiny doesn't equate with money. The only reason for a child of God to have money is to help with destiny. *First Thessalonians 5: 24* says, *"Faithful is He that calleth you, Who also will do it."* You don't have to carry the load. Let go, and let God work in and through you. All He wants you to do is to be a willing vessel of His love. *Revelation 12: 11* reads, *"And they overcame him by the blood of the Lamb, and by the word of their testimony; and they loved not their lives unto the death."*

Enthos is a Greek word which means in God. The word enthusiasm comes from this Greek word. Therefore, if you are enthusiastic about something, you are in God, assuming that you are enthusiastic about something that is for the good of all people concerned. Enthusiasm is what sells. People love to be around those who are excited about life and what it has to offer. However, there is a fine line between enthusiasm and being overly anxious. When we are overly anxious, we are usually in the flesh and thinking about our own selfish interests instead of the interests of others. All of us want basically the same things. We all would certainly like to be financially independent, wouldn't we? It is okay to dream. Don't ever let anyone tell you that it isn't. However, it is not okay to dream if that is all you ever do. You must learn to take action. Faith demands that action be taken. Faith is what God honors. There could be a number of things holding you back. Are you afraid of success? This is one I am dealing with at the present time. I have decided to go on with Jesus anyway and to work through this fear, just as I have all my life with the other fears. I feel like I have conquered the fear of rejection from so many years of selling insurance, carpet, and furniture. I have overcome the fear of getting up in front of a crowd and talking simply by doing it. I have overcome the fear of singing a solo, even songs I have written, simply by doing it. No, I'm not the greatest singer in the world. However, the good Lord sends me lyrics to the songs. Don't you think He expects me to share them with others, or do you think He sends them to me just to keep to myself? I don't think so. He said to make a joyful noise to the Lord. All He wants is a willing vessel for His love to flow through. You don't have to be perfect. You never will be perfect. We are, however, supposed to strive to be perfect by keeping our eyes on Jesus. He is the symbol with which we can gauge our success.

We must never resent other people's success or be jealous of the money they have. I can't stress this enough. That is one sure way to keep God's blessings from flowing to us. The Bible says in *Proverbs 15: 15* that *"He that is of a merry heart hath a continual feast."* Some people might say, "I would be happy too if I had his money." That's not the way things work. You must choose to be happy first, then the blessings of God will come. You will become very happy when you learn to fully embrace the love of Jesus for yourself. Then God's love will flow out of you to others with no effort of your own. It happens automatically. If you have a burning desire to do something, then the chances are that God gave you that desire. He is trying to help you give birth to something probably far greater than you can imagine. Just stay close to the Lord. Keep praying for wisdom and direction every day and watch your destiny unfold before you. Learn to focus and to concentrate. Set goals for yourself. Give yourself deadlines. Be realistic with your plans, and never give up; be persistent. Use creative visualization. You must picture yourself in a given situation before it will ever happen. Learn to be grateful for what you have and to be a good steward of what God has already given to you. Remember that if you have accepted Jesus into your heart and made Him your Lord and Savior, then you have been redeemed from the curse of the law. Old things have passed away, and all things have become new. Remember that God has removed your sins from you as far as the east is from the west, and that's a long way. He has wiped your slate clean. You are a new creation; don't ever forget that. Don't allow Satan to tell you otherwise. Know that Satan does not respect you; he does, however, respect authority, and you have been given authority in the name of Jesus. Resist the devil, and he will flee from you. You must dare to be different. Learn to think big. Prayer is where the action is. Pray often and be diligent. Hearken to the Word of God; His Word is there for you to use. *Ecclesiastes 9: 10a* says, *"Whatsoever thy hand findeth to do, do it with thy might,"* and according to *Matthew 6: 21, "For where your treasure is, there will your heart be also."* Let the fruits of the Spirit shine forth in and through you: love, joy, peace, longsuffering, gentleness, goodness, faith, meekness, and temperance. *Proverbs 4: 23* reminds us to *"Keep thy heart with all diligence; for out of it are the issues of life."*

Zig Ziglar said, "If you help enough other people get what they want, then you will get what you want. That's what life is all about, and we all want the same things. What we give away will come back to us. You cannot outgive God, no matter how hard you may try. *Luke 6: 38a* has this to say about giving: *"Give, and it shall be given unto you; good measure, pressed down, and shaken together, and running over, shall men give into your bosom."* I know you sometimes wonder if God truly loves you unconditionally. I pray that the following Scriptures will answer this question for you once and for all:

Romans 5: 8: "But God commendeth His love toward us, in that, while we were yet sinners, Christ died for us."

How much more than that one act does it take for God to prove His love for us?

John 3: 16: "For God so loved the world, that He gave His only begotten Son, that whosoever believeth in Him should not perish, but have everlasting life."

Do *you* love anyone enough to sacrifice your only child for them?

1 John 3: 1: "Behold, what manner of love the Father hath bestowed upon us, that we should be called the sons of God: therefore the world knoweth us not, because it knew Him not."

I would say that God is pretty proud of us to be calling us His sons (of course He means daughters, too).

1 John 4: 8: "He that loveth not knoweth not God, for God is love."

John 17: 24: "Father, I will that they also, whom Thou has given Me, be with Me where I am; that they may behold My glory, which Thou hast given Me: for Thou lovedst Me before the foundation of the world."

This was Jesus talking to our heavenly Father.

Matthew 6: 25-26: "Therefore I say unto you, Take no thought for your life, what ye shall eat, or what ye shall drink; nor yet for your body, what ye shall put on. Is not the life more than meat, and the body than raiment? Behold the fowls of the air: for they sow not, neither do they reap, nor gather into barns; yet your heavenly Father feedeth them. Are ye not much better than they?"

This is Jesus talking, also. In other words, we are not to worry about anything. God sees and knows all of our needs. We must believe that He will meet those needs before they will be met. Struggling, complaining, kicking, screaming, and pulling your hair out are all unnecessary. Just choose to believe that God loves you and that He has always met all your needs, and He always will. However, He wants to do much more than that.

Hebrews 13: 5: "Let your conversation be without covetousness; and be content with such things as ye have: for He hath said, I will never leave thee, nor forsake thee."

God is always right there with us wherever we are. He said to be still and know that He is God. Turn your eyes upon Jesus in the midst of your struggle and watch how your troubles just grow strangely dim, just like the song says.

Hebrews 12: 5-6: "And ye have forgotten the exhortation which speaketh unto you as unto children, My son, despise not thou the chastening of the Lord, nor faint when thou art rebuked of Him: For whom the Lord chasteneth, and scourgeth every son whom He receiveth."

Just as any earthly father who loves his children corrects his children, then so does our heavenly Father. He will not let us just get away with anything and everything. When you are feeling guilty about something, this is the Holy Spirit dealing with you and encouraging you to repent, to make things right. Whatever you need to do, you will be guided by the Holy Spirit. When you follow those promptings of the Holy Spirit, you will feel like a million dollars because the guilt will be gone. The weight of the guilt is not worth carrying around. Pride makes a very lonely person, and it will surely keep you cut off from God's blessings.

When you are learning how to control the good things in life rather than always riding on the coattails of other people's thoughts and actions, then this will become the most exciting journey you have ever encountered. This is where you find joy. You must learn to love yourself first before you can release the inner self. Embracing positive attitudes and creative energies helps us overcome fear and develops confidence. Joy in the highest meaning of the word entails an encounter with God. Joy becomes the power of God's grace. We become full of joy as we learn more and more how to trust God. We maintain that joy as we accept Christ at His word and emulate His lifestyle in every situation. Being a witness in testimony is a key to keeping our joy. We become joyful when we know that we are bringing light into dark places. What we have experienced in the past can be used either to help us progress into confidences or regress into fear and anxiety. In *2 Corinthians 2: 13* we read, *"Now thanks be unto God, which always causeth us to triumph in Christ, and maketh manifest the savour of His knowledge by us in every place."* We breed the fruits of the Spirit when we learn to speak words of joy and kindness. The spiritual life must become our highest priority in order to maintain joy. *Nehemiah 8: 10* says that *"the joy of the Lord is your strength."* When faith increases, so does happiness. Therefore, doesn't it make sense that we need to do what is necessary to be ever increasing our faith? This is done by hearing and hearing and hearing the Word. We can't experience too much hearing. The way that we use our time determines how happy and joyful we are. We are the happiest when we are being productive. Learn to manage your time wisely. We don't know how much we have left, do we? We should strive to meet the challenge of *Philippians 3: 13b-14: "Forgetting those things which are behind, and reaching forth unto those things which are before. I press toward the mark for the prize of the high calling of God in Christ Jesus."*

How you see yourself determines how you live and what you accomplish. When Christians begin to believe in themselves, they will begin to change the way the world sees the followers of Christ. We need to examine our own self-image and see how it differs from how God sees us. God has placed certain desires in your heart, and if He placed them there, then I can promise you that He can bring them into fruition. You must be persistent and determined. If you are constantly comparing yourself to other people, stop right now. You are a unique individual, and God does not want you to be exactly like anyone else. You are special. He created you with unique abilities and talents, and He expects you to develop them and to use them for His glory. This does not necessarily mean that He wants you to be a preacher or a teacher of the Word. We need Christians in every walk of life, truck drivers to politicians and everything in between. Quit looking to other people for your happiness. Your happiness does not depend on what someone else does or does not do. Your happiness in life depends on no one other than yourself and the choices you make, so stop blaming others. There is no value in it. Choose to forgive. Get over what has been eating you up inside. Just simply decide to let it go. You have analyzed it to death. You have made yourself miserable. Aren't you tired of doing that? In order to experience anything different, you must do something different. As long as you continue to do the same things, you will get the same results.

What have you allowed people to label you with, or what box have you allowed people to put you into? Learn what you need to do to get yourself out of that box. Find out the true desires of your heart. Find out what dreams you have that can be developed and what you can do to put those dreams into action. You must speak words of faith behind those dreams. Even with all the present-day revelation of faith and all the talk about releasing faith, standing on faith, and believing God in faith, we do not hear very much discussion on trust. A lack of trust in God is at the bottom of all our problems and difficulties. A lack of trust is one of the major results of low self-esteem. When you feel badly about yourself, you do not trust. When you can't trust God, you feel badly about your-self, so you get into a cycle of doubting and not trusting. You can make it a habit to affirm this every day. Try repeating this phrase: "I trust in the Lord with all my heart, and I lean not unto my own understanding. I acknowledge Him in all my ways, and He directs my path." Making small, but powerful, changes in your life slowly but surely will bring about a world of difference in your life. Rome wasn't built in a day. Don't even try. God has a perfect plan for your life. You don't have to be a carbon copy of someone else. Let the purpose of your life unfold to you as you develop your relationship with the Lord and as you bask in the awesome, wonderful experience of resting in His love. You can be free from fear, which is indeed the most crippling disease on the face of this earth.

Fear of failure and fear of rejection are the two primary fears people deal with, so let's address those. Take the fear of failure, for example. If we never take a risk, then we are never attempting anything because everything requires risk to a certain degree. There are no sure-fire, ironclad guarantees that what we are attempting or going to attempt will be a success. However, one thing is certain. If we don't try, we will never know if some good idea or plan would have worked. How do you define success? Success means different things to different people. As a couple of hypothetical examples, Joe Smith could be referred to as being successful because he has worked his way up the corporate ladder and now holds a prestigious executive position with XYZ

Company. It's irrelevant to some people who look at Joe as a success that he has a drinking problem, a less than harmonious marriage, and has experienced many health problems, including two heart attacks.

On the other hand, let's look at Sue Jones. She is a wife of ten years, has two happy, healthy children, and is married to a loving man who works as a mechanic. They live in a modest, three-bedroom house. Occasionally, it gets a little messy with their children and with family, friends, and neighbors dropping in. However, their home is filled with love and joy, and on any given day you can stop by their home and feel welcome and appreciated. Now, wouldn't you say that Sue and her husband are both successful? We are never defeated unless we say we are. Actually, failure is never final, and success is never ending.

Now let's analyze the fear of rejection. Only by learning to wholly accept ourselves as we are right now can we accept others as they are right now and be free from rejection. How then do we learn to accept ourselves? We simply make a firm decision to accept what God says in His Word about us. He loves us just as we are right now, but He longs to become more intimate with us so that He can shower us with blessings. We are all operating on different levels of awareness. The level of awareness that we are on depends on how much truth we are admitting to ourselves about ourselves. Of course, we all slip and stumble, but we pick up ourselves, dust off ourselves, and start all over again. When we quit picking ourselves up and trying again, then we really can be classified as a complete failure. Sometimes you just need a little breather. Sometimes you just need to rest in God, seeking Him and a much deeper relationship with Him. You don't have to be so busy all the time. That is not what I am talking about.

If freedom requires self-analyzation, then of course we must now deal with guilt. The sin nature of man has been engrained into the human brain since Adam and Eve first disobeyed God, which resulted in guilt. According to *Romans 3: 23, "For all have sinned, and come short of the glory of God."* There is no one on the face of this earth who has not done something for which he/she has been extremely ashamed. The Bible says that we are born into sin. Someone told me recently that he believed that we are born into this world as innocent children and that we learn to be evil from others. That is not what God's Word says; it is just the opposite. We are prone to sin and to wander. That's why we need a Savior. That's why we so desperately need Jesus. That's why we need the Word of God to break the yokes of bondage off of us. The Bible tells us in *Romans 12: 2, "And be not con-*

formed to this world: but be ye transformed by the renewing of your mind..."

An engram is a lasting memory of an incident that occurred in the past. These memories are deeply embedded in our subconscious minds. However, they are still very active in our present lives, or at least in most people's lives. Many times when we are least expecting it, we can be engaged in a set of circumstances and something someone says, usually a spouse, will just seemingly for no reason upset us to no end. The engram from the past came into play, causing us to react the way we did to that person. Something they did reminded us so much of the other person in our past, and we obviously had not learned to forgive that other person. How then can the present relationship be a healthy one? It is difficult. We must learn to forgive. Forgiveness is not an option. It is mandatory if we want to be truly happy. We must learn to make our minds come under complete subjection to our hearts. Out of the heart come all the issues of life. We learn to transform our minds by quoting God's Word, and those words sink down into our hearts. This does not happen overnight; it is an ongoing process if we want to be transformed into the person that God wants us to be. With that said, I reluctantly use the word religion or religious because I am not religious, but I do have a close personal relationship with

Jesus. However, every religion teaches positive affirmations. The following ones, which could be used frequently, are wonderful and could be written on three by five cards and carried with you. All of them come from the Bible:

"Greater is He that is in me than he that is in the world."

"His grace is sufficient for me."

"Whatsoever things are pure, whatsoever things are lovely, whatsoever things are just, think upon these things."

"God has not given me a spirit of fear, but of love, and power, and a strong mind."

"No weapon formed against me shall prosper."

"I fear no evil for Thou art with me."

"Let the words of my mouth and the meditation of my heart be acceptable in Thy sight, Oh Lord, my strength and my redeemer."

"The Lord is my Shepherd, I shall not want."

"Jesus came that I might have life and that I might have it more abundantly."

"I can do all things through Christ Who strengthens me."

Yes, God wants you to personalize His promises. That's why they are in the Bible. That's what they are for. Learn to do that, and watch your faith soar!! Watch what happens when you begin to believe what God says about you!! A whole new world will open up for you. Little miracles will begin to happen. It will not be your own strength but God working in and through you, so be careful. Always give Him the glory, and He will give you the victory.

Pleasing God as a believer is based on one truth: total and complete dependence on the Lord. This is a key element to living a victorious Christian life. The following Scriptures affirm that fact:

Ephesians 2: 8-10: "For by grace are ye saved through faith; and that not of yourselves: it is the gift of God: Not of works, lest any man should boast. For we are His workmanship, created in Christ Jesus unto good works, which God hath before ordained that we should walk in them."

Ephesians 5: 2a: "And walk in love, as Christ also hath loved us."

Ephesians 5: 8: "For ye were sometimes darkness, but now are ye light in the Lord: walk as children of light."

We walk as children of light by bringing those heavenly places into our earthly surroundings, by allowing our light to shine among men. Paul tells us in *Ephesians 3: 20, "Now unto Him that is able to do exceeding abundantly above all that we ask or think, according to the power that worketh in us.*" These heavenly places are a place of power and might. That mighty, mighty power is already inside of you. God wants you to display it to those around you. Don't let the enemy intimidate you or steal from you. Christ gained the victory; all you have to do is maintain it. *Romans 8: 37* declares, *"Nay, in all these things we are more than conquerors through Him that loved us."* A conqueror is already victorious. You aren't just a conqueror; you are more than a conqueror. Today you do not fight for victory; you fight from a position of victory (the work on Calvary 2,000 years ago).

JESUS HAS WON!!

STAND IN THE VICTORY!!

YOU ARE MORE THAN A CONQUEROR THROUGH HIM THAT LOVES YOU!!

BELIEVE IT!

ADDENDUM

This is December, 2010, and as we go to press I just thought you may like to have an update concerning my life in the last year or so and how God's plan continues to unfold for me.

I really didn't know if I would ever be married again or not, having received a PhD in "How Not To Have A Successful Marriage" from the University of Hard Knocks or even if I should have ever gotten married in the first place. With all the emotional turmoil I went through from such poor choices in the past, along with my personal emotional baggage, chances seemed mighty slim I could ever find a man who would now even begin to come close to my NEW and VERY HIGH standards.

But, God is so good. After twelve years of being single, I realized that in the past I had never asked God to provide the husband He wanted for me. So, I began to pray for a man with specific characteristics, and trust me, the description was lengthy. I certainly couldn't afford to make another wrong choice of my own. Within two months Dwayne appeared. He came into the furniture store and six months later we were married. God is good, all the time. His plans are always so much better than our own. I am happier now than I ever dreamed of being. I truly have the favor of God, and it is working in every area of my life. It is all about believing in what God can do in you, for you, and through you, as you learn to get yourself off your mind and onto the things that God is interested in.

The house I lived in for years was listed with a Real Estate Agency for over a year. Finally, I began to get specific with my prayer for the right buyer and within four days the agent called and said, "We have a cash buyer for the house," yes, even in this crazy market with only one out of every three-hundred houses selling right now. Glory to God. The kicker is that if it had been a financed deal, we would have all had to jump through a whole bunch of hoops in order to satisfy a lender. A cash sale was perfect.

As for my two sons, Paris is now 45 years old and I will be performing the marriage ceremony for him and Bobbie at our precious little church, Pleasant Ridge United Methodist in Enterprise, Alabama on Valentine's Day, February 14,

2011. I am so grateful that he has received all of God's love for himself and has forgiven himself to the degree that he is now able to have a blessed relationship with a wonderful young lady who is a registered nurse and who has an eleven year old daughter, as well as two grown sons out on their own. By the way, my grand-daughter-to-be is a straight A student. I will meet her for the first time Christmas, next week, and I have had a ball shopping for her. I don't believe in coincidence, but my son, Brent, who lives in Hawaii, will be going to Orlando March 3rd for his girlfriend's friend's wedding. I believe God is working it all out so that he can be here for his brother's wedding. GOD'S FAVOR IS FOR THOSE WHO LOVE AND TRUST HIM!!!

ON THE FOLLOWING PAGES I AM
SHARING A FEW OF THE POEMS
AND SONGS I HAVE WRITTEN
THROUGH THE YEARS.
I PRAY YOU WILL BE BLESSED.

IN THE MIDST OF MY REBELLION

I learned about You as a child
I accepted You as my Lord and Savior
However, not too many years later
I wandered off into the wilderness
Even in the midst of my rebellion
I sometimes felt Your presence
It was the essence of Your being
My heart was surely longing for
I seemed to sense within my spirit
There must be more to life
Than what my present experience
Afforded me at that time and place
You invaded my space
Even in the midst of my rebellion
I didn't know of any plan
That You could have for me
But, I could see You had no
Intentions of leaving me alone
The songs we used to sing
Would sometimes infiltrate my mind
Jesus Loves Me would ring loudly

In my ears and my fears would

Somehow subside, if even for a short time

In the midst of my rebellion

Glenda Carlson

*I wrote this poem in 2006 as I was reflecting back on many years prior to that when I was around twenty-five years old.

THE TRUTH

The Holy Spirit's the greatest teacher of all.

I feel I must share some things with you all

About the truth which can possibly set us all free.

Here's the truth as the Spirit revealed it to me.

The Kingdom of God we must all seek first,

For the Word we should develop an unquenchable thirst.

When we want wisdom as much as air we breathe

Then and only then will wisdom we receive.

Words are the most powerful force ever to be.

Man alone cannot tame a tongue that flaps loosely.

There's life and death in the power of the tongue.

There's too many sad songs even yet to be sung.

Christians hold themselves in bondage, constantly speaking

Of troubles and woes when it's faith we're all seeking.

The opposite of faith of course we all know is fear.

Fear filled words are not what God wants to hear.

Jesus died on the cross to save us from our sin.

Let's let go of anger and invite Jesus in.

Yes, you are worthy of God's infinite love

And your share of blessings He shines from above.

They're yours for the asking if you only believe.

Jesus died on the cross for you and me.

By His stripes we are healed from all sickness and pain.

Thank God for the power in Jesus' name.

1987 Reverend Glenda Carlson

* After I received the Baptism of the Holy Spirit on October, 1987 on a Sunday afternoon, the Holy Spirit woke me up the next morning at five o'clock with the words to the above poem.

DADDY'S BIBLE

1ST VERSE

When I'm alone and weary and I have nowhere to turn
I pick up my Daddy's Bible for I have much to learn.
I read these tear stained pages and they remind me he's
gone,
But he left me his Bible so I would not be alone.

2nd VERSE

Sometimes when life seems empty and people hard to
understand
I pick up Daddy's Bible, asking God to reveal His plan.
I focus upon His written Word and peace comes over me.
Because of Daddy's Bible I'm not blind now - I can see.

CHORUS

And I remember Daddy sittin' in that 'ole brown chair
Reading through the Word of God of His love and how
He cares.

He kept his Bible handy and read it every day.

Thank God for Daddy's Bible – for He showed me the way.

1988 Reverend Glenda Carlson

* This was the first Christian song I ever wrote. This was in the Spring of 1988. I sang this song to Mother once when I was visiting her several years after Daddy had died. She said "You've never written me a song," so on the way back home to Atlanta I asked the Lord to send me the words to a song for her. After crying all the way back home, the birth of a very special song entitled *I'll Always Love You Dear Momma* emerged.

I'LL ALWAYS LOVE YOU DEAR MOMMA

1ST VERSE

Momma used to comb my hair in Shirley Temple curls;

People always said I was such a lucky girl.

A blue crepe paper dress she made for me in second grade,

In our school play I was her star wearing the dress she

made.

She worked part time so I could have Christmas like

my friends.

She'd buy me clothes and toys and things,

Sometimes old clothes she'd mend.

2nd VERSE

I was just eighteen years old when I first left home,

Thinking I was old enough to be out on my own.

Momma didn't try to stop me but tears were in her eyes,

And every time I go home now and leave she always cries.

Driving home I long to be a little girl again,

So that Momma could tuck me in bed like she did then.

But it's back to city life and facing the whole world.

It's hard being a woman feeling like a little girl.

CHORUS

And I'll always love you dear Momma,

Though I've never told you enough.

Yes, I'll always love you dear Momma,

This song's my gift for you to show my love.

TAG

And I'll always love you dear Momma.

1991 Reverend Glenda Carlson

* I wrote this song in 1991 and sent it to my mother for Mother's Day on a cassette. She cried of course. I sang this song in our church on Mother's Day, 1998. There didn't seem to be a dry eye in the church. We all love our mothers dearly, don't we?

I'M FREE

1ST VERSE

I tried for years, the good Lord knows;

I tried to make it on my own.

Cried many tears and suffered guilt

For the things that I'd done wrong.

I thought this earthly love I share

Would somehow ease all the pain.

Since you came into my life

I have never been the same.

2nd VERSE

You took my fears – You took my doubts

And Filled my heart with Your sweet love,

And it flows from deep within.

As You pour it from above

You give me strength from day to day,

And the courage to go on.

I'll meet You someday in the sky

And we'll go to our Heavenly Home.

CHORUS

You give me joy – You give me love.

You give me peace in my soul.

You set me free – made me believe.

Lord, You've made me whole.

Now I can share the love You give

With others I see – praise God for His love.

I'm Free

1992 Reverend Glenda Carlson

* I wrote this song in 1992. I sing it as a love song to Jesus.

WRAPPED IN GOD'S LOVE

1ST VERSE

Confusion surrounded every move that I made.

I must have been taking much more than I gave.

So restless inside in every thought that I had,

With a smile on my face, but inside I was so sad.

2nd VERSE

I was just living a life filled with sin;

No peace did I have without or within.

Just drifting along with no hope in sight,

Something happened – I was drawn into the light.

3rd VERSE

All my fears and doubts seemed to be all gone

As God put new words in my heart for a song.

Words to exalt Him and His power on high,

He lives in my heart, let my words seek to Him glorify

4th VERSE

Through God's eyes of love I looked all around,

No doubt in my heart – I am heaven bound.

For I have been saved only by His precious grace

Someday I'll see Him – I'll see Jesus face to face.

CHORUS

I was wrapped in God's love from my head to my toe,

From His precious love I'll never let go.

The love that I felt flowing over me

Words can't describe adequately.

As I opened my heart and let Jesus in

His blood and my tears washed away all my sin.

And I heard Him tell me from His throne above

My child, you are Mine and you're wrapped in My love.

1998 Reverend Glenda Carlson

* I wrote this song 1-18-98. I suppose I was remembering when I had received the Baptism of the Holy Spirit in October of 1987.

HELP MY UNBELIEF

Let me not grow weary
In my prayers to You.
Take not Your Spirit from me,
Whatever You do.
Help me when I stumble
To get back up again.
Help me be quick
Lord to repent
Of all my dark sin.

CHORUS

Lead me and guide me
Throughout every day.
Wherever I go
I pray You will show
Me what to say.

Let people see Jesus
Shining through me.
Increase my faith

Day after day;

Help my unbelief.

1998 Reverend Glenda Carlson

* I wrote this song June 3, 1998. This was around the same time that Paris was going through such a hard time with his father, and my heart seemed to be breaking into for him, his father, and yes, for Sharon, also. Even as close as I am to the Lord I still went through a wide gamut of emotions when I found out she had killed Paris' father. Wayne was my first love. I was eighteen years old when I met him and I worshipped the ground he walked on. I cannot in my own human strength forgive her. I prayed so hard for so many years for total healing between Paris and his father. Only because Jesus lives in my heart can I forgive her. I pray that she can find peace in her heart and accept the cleansing, forgiving power of our Lord and Savior, Jesus Christ.

VESSELS OF GOLD

1ST VERSE

God gives us choices;

We know right from wrong.

He knows we're not perfect,

He can make us strong.

And it's in the valleys

We look deep within

And let go of our pride,

And confess all our sin.

2nd VERSE

And only in fire

Is gold purified.

And it's in the fire

God burns away pride.

We need a Savior

To carry us through,

With His arms around us,

Showing us what to do.

CHORUS

And God has a plan

For woman and man.

But it's up to us

To learn how to trust.

He peels back the pain;

He sifts out the shame,

Removes all our fears.

He wipes away tears,

Fills us with His love,

Brings us back in the fold.

He saves our soul

When we go astray.

There's a price we must pay.

He's making vessels of gold.

1998 Reverend Glenda Carlson

* I wrote this song 6-18-98. This was also around the same time that Paris was having such a difficult time. My being able to write songs has helped me to deal with all my heart-aches, watching people I love suffer from being unhappy.

SOMETIMES IT TAKES TIME

FIRST VERSE

Sometimes it takes time to be honest with myself;

When I want truth and I won't settle for nothing less.

I turn and go deep within,

And I can see all my sin.

CHORUS

I seek a Power outside myself,

Reach for a Strong Hand to hold on to,

Look for a Bright Light upon my path.

I know Jesus will see me through.

SECOND VERSE

Sometimes it takes time to be willing to let go.

I want freedom, but there's a price to pay I know.

I dig deep within my heart,

And I have known from the start.

CHORUS

I need a Power outside myself.

I need a Strong Hand to hold on to.

I need a Bright Light upon my path.

I need Jesus to see me through.

BRIDGE

I need shelter from the storm.

I need to feel safe from all harm.

I need a Savior to rescue me.

I need to feel His love for me.

REPEAT CHORUS

TAG

Sometimes it takes time

But I always

Feel His love.

Sometimes it takes time.

Sometimes it takes time.

Sometimes it takes time.

Sometimes it takes time.

Sometimes it takes time. Sometimes it takes time.

Sometimes it takes time. Sometimes it takes time.

1999 Reverend Glenda Carlson

* The Lord gave me the lyrics and melody to this song on the way back home to Dothan from the Jazz Festival in New Orleans on 4-29-99.

CPSIA information can be obtained
at www.ICGtesting.com
Printed in the USA
LVOW12s0301270816
502049LV00001B/2/P